Seeing Stars®

Nanci Bell

Symbol Imagery for Phonemic Awareness, Sight Words and Spelling

The letters of language are like the stars in the Universe-parts of a whole.

Illustrations: Phyllis Lindamood

Design Consultant: Pierre Rademaker

©1997, 2001 Nanci Bell
Gander Educational Publishing®
412 Higuera Street, Suite 200
San Luis Obispo, California 93401
(800) 554-1819 • (805) 541-5523

ISBN 0-945-856-06-7

Acknowledgements

The many faces of the students that stared at little colored blocks must be thanked; out of their pain, the concept of symbol imagery became a reality. The hearts of many clinicians and associates must be acknowledged as they tried this or that technique; out of their patience, the stimulation of symbol imagery became a reality.

Special acknowledgments go to: 1) my daughter, Alison, who *loves* symbol imagery and presented gains in spelling as a result of its diligent use with students, 2) my son, Rodney, who forever and ever quietly helps his mother in all endeavors, 3) Paul Worthington, who gives constant support to my life's work, 4) Dr. Al Paivio, who gave life to dual coding theory and thus conceptual breadth to my work, 5) to Phyllis Lindamood, who brings laughter and reason to all our lives, and 5) Pat Lindamood, who first showed me how to track sounds on blocks without stacking them.

To Rhett

Perhaps they are not the stars…
but openings in heaven
where the love of our lost ones pours through
to let us know they are happy.

Inuit Poem

The letters of language
are like the stars in the Universe—
parts of a whole.

Preface

I am writing this book to an unknown "you" that seems to live in my imagination—almost heavenly in shape. Sometimes you are a teacher, sometimes a parent, sometimes a group of teachers from the "back table" in a class I recently taught, sometimes a sea of faces from an entire class, or sometimes a student who may benefit from this work. No matter who the "you" is on a given day or a given moment, I have the constant presence of my mother and my beautiful, bright son—smiling at me and encouraging me to stay at the keyboard, no *fits* allowed.

The pages of this book contain theory and techniques to practice a very important aspect of cognition. As a lead goose, getting tired, keep this going. Don't let symbol imagery become a stepchild to whatever new fad comes along in education. There are truths in life, and the need for imaging in comprehension, and imaging in reading and spelling words, is one of those truths. And, anyone can learn to do it. Anyone can be a champ in a spelling bee. Anyone can learn to memorize sight words. Anyone can learn to read fluently and confidently in context. Anyone can walk up stairs and rattle off letters in a word at the same time. It is all a matter of integrating imagery with language, dual coding.

I hope you read this with the feeling of love and respect that I give to you. You can do this. You can do anything.

Nanci Bell
January 1997

The Contents

The Concept

The Process

The Summary

The Appendix

The Concept

1

"TEEOHEMOHDOUBLEAUROHDOUBLEYOU" or Listen Nanci

A Mystery of Years Ago

Sitting in the living room in front of the fire, school work piled around me, I heard my mother coming into the hall, then heading for the stairs. Now was a good time to ask her; then I wouldn't have to look it up in the dictionary. She can spell anything.

"Mom, how do you spell "tomorrow?"

Her footsteps never missing a beat, she rattled off some sort of rapid, foreign speech, "TEEOHEMOHDOUBLEAUROHDOUBLEYOU."

Eyes blinking and searching the universe for some sense, I said, "WHAT?"

As she crested the top of the stairs, Martian speech came at me again, "TEEOHEMOHDOUBLEAUROHDOUBLEYOU."

Panicking, I yelled, "Wait Mom, I can't get that. What did you say? T what?"

Footsteps came to a stop. I could picture her red hair and pretty-but-determined face as she turned toward me. "Listen Nanci. Pay attention."

Why did I have to ask? Then in somewhat slower speech, I heard a careful, slightly impatient, "TEE-OH-EM-OH-DOUBLEAUR-OH-DOUBLE-YOU."

The haze starting to clear, images started to form, the Martian speech suddenly converted to my language. Oh, she meant T-O-M-O, but what was that letter coming after the O? What is a DOUBLEAUR? Is that like a W? Then, I got it. Perception occurred. The haze was gone. Lucidity at last! She was saying a double R! Two R's! Then an O. Then a W. T-O-M-O-R-R-O-W. I saw it.

Quickly, I wrote it down before I lost it. Regaining my intellectual status with my mother suddenly became very important. "T-O-M-O-R-R-O-W. Thanks Mom, I have it."

Unfortunately, her foot steps didn't become fainter, instead they started coming back down the stairs. Uh-oh. In the hall, now the living room. Head down, Nanci. Keep your head down.

She was standing over me. "Nanci, how are you doing in spelling?"

Quick response, Nanci. Be confident. Fourth grade is easy. Show no fear or the lecture will start again. Why did I have to ask her for help? What was I thinking? "Fine, Mom. I get A's all the time. Hundreds. Every test. It's easy for me."

Too late, here it came. "Well, if they'd go back to teaching phonics in school, and doing spelling bees, kids wouldn't have problems learning to read and spell. When I was in school, we had to learn the sounds for the letters, and that helped us sound out words, but we also did spelling bees. That's why I can spell so well. Kids didn't have problems learning to read and spell like they do now. Why don't you have to do spelling bees anymore?"

"Uh, I don't know Mom." Head down. Keep your head down.

Undaunted, she continued in her usual passionate way. "Listen to me Nanci, we had to do spelling bees. We learned to sound out words and we also learned to see the words in our head. I just can't understand why they don't do that anymore."

Vowing never, ever, to ask her to spell a word for me again, I muttered, "I don't know Mom." I'll never ask her again. I swear I'll look it up. I swear.

I could feel her waiting for more, looking up at her, seeing her intensity, I sputtered, "We just don't do that, Mom. But, I can sound out words." (I had taught myself "phonics" by noting that certain letters in certain words seemed to make certain sounds.) Please let this be over.

Sighing, she stayed for a few more seconds, then gave up and headed for the stairs to resume her mom-mission.

Never. I would never ask her again. Anyhow I can never really understand her. Just yesterday I asked her how to spell the word *necessary*. Her response was a rapid N-E-C-E-double-S-A-R-Y. How does she get those letters out of her mouth that fast? And, why can't I get them in my head at the same rate that she says them? And, for heavens sake, why can't I get that double thing she does? What a mystery.

Oh, well. I'll think about this tomorrow.

What is Symbol Imagery?

Tomorrow's Lesson

My mom taught me many lessons about life, very pragmatic lessons. Early on, the first I remember was that I had some disease called, *"Overlysensitive."* Enough said. Another was, *"Work never hurt anyone. When you've got problems—work. Do anything. Wash windows, mop floors, do anything to keep busy."* (Always suspicious that she was just trying to get me to clean my room, I didn't take that one seriously until much later in life.) Translated: Get your mind off your troubles and yourself—be outside yourself rather than inside yourself. Another was, *"Everyone is wrapped up in their own ball of yarn."* Translated: People have their own agenda. Don't get your feelings hurt. Another was, *"It's OK for people to be different. It would be a terrible world if everyone was the same."* Translated: Have respect and tolerance for others. Another was, *"We should be teaching phonics and spelling bees. It doesn't make any sense not to!"*

As I move through life, my mother's wisdom has served me well, often recalled just in the nick of time to help me through a learning experience. But, her commentary about symbol imagery, though buried for years, is a lesson I have been able to give to others. Returning through the mist, it has been instrumental in helping children and adults solve the mystery of reading and spelling.

Years ago, there was a moment of lucidity that resurrected the t-o-m-o-double-r-o-w experience and endless head shaking. Sharing a private clinical practice with Pat Lindamood, I was helping children and adults, some labeled severe dyslexics, learn to read and spell. The program we were using, the Lindamood® Auditory Discrimination in Depth (ADD) Program, has individuals *feel* sounds in their mouths and use that *feeling* to track sounds in words. One day, after many practice sessions of tracking, I realized that the students who were reaching automaticity in that task were also *seeing* the corresponding letters in their minds. They didn't have to use articulatory feedback any more because they were *seeing* the changes; they could make accurate changes very quickly, the outward sign that their phonemic awareness was becoming established. I noted a relationship between how automatically/rapidly they perceived the change and their ability to *see the letters*. I also noted that those same students began to acquire sight words more readily and so could read in context more smoothly; they self-corrected more easily. In general, they were nearing the end of intervention.

I thought about the relevancy of this *seeing* of the letters. Could it be that seeing letters in the mind's eye would help individuals track sounds? Could stimulating it sooner help develop phonemic awareness more quickly? Could it be that seeing those letters would enable students to move through the ADD program more quickly? Could being able to image the letters help someone in the "hold and compare" task necessary for self-correcting? Could the ability to visualize letters be stimulated? Would that enable us to improve spelling beyond "phonetically correct representations?" Could it be that imaging letters is a different cognitive task than imaging concepts? Is that why there seems to be a dichotomy in imagery available to individuals: 1) concept imagery for those who can primarily image concepts and are good comprehenders, but poor spellers, and 2) symbol imagery for those who can primarily image letters and are good spellers, but not good comprehenders? Is there a parts-to-whole issue in sensory processing? Was this a critical missing piece not only in the development of phonemic awareness, but in the development of sight word recognition and, therefore, fluent contextual reading? Was my mother right? Again?

Symbol Imagery

Symbol imagery is the ability to visualize letters in words. Seeing letters in the mind's eye is symbol imagery. Experience it for yourself by picturing a lesson with me. I'm saying—

"What do you see when I say the nonsense word "*fip*."

Look away. I know you just read the word, but take a moment and try to see the letters in your imagination.

"Now change *fip* to *fap*."

Look away to hear me say it so you can see it. You probably put up a different set of letters on your imaged screen or you saw the letter **i** go out and the letter **a** come in.

"Now change *fap* to *frap*."

Look away to see and hear me. Did you see the **r** come in right after the **f**?

It is difficult to do this exercise by reading it, but try to experience it again.

"What do you see when I say the real word *enough*?"

Look away to see and hear me. What letters do you see? Try saying them backwards.

If you could do this exercise in your imagination, you were *experiencing* symbol imagery—the ability to visualize letters. It may have been easy or difficult for you, or somewhere in between, but in any case, skill in this area is not related to your intelligence! For the last six years, researching symbol imagery and creating steps for developing it, I have given a similar exercise to more than five hundred educational professionals, primarily speech pathologists and teachers. The exercise/questionnaire consists of a Likert scale in which individuals rate their own abilities in symbol imagery, phonemic awareness, and spelling, followed by a sample of one through five syllable nonsense words to spell. In analyzing the information, there is a direct correlation between how the professionals rate their symbol imagery, their phonemic awareness, and their spelling ability, with their tested ability to phonetically spell nonsense words. For example, in general, if they rated themselves high in symbol imagery and phonemic awareness, they rated themselves high in spelling, and were also good phonetic spellers—getting all the sounds and syllables in the right place. The reverse was also true. If they rated themselves poor in symbol imagery and phonemic awareness, they also rated themselves poor in spelling, and their ability to phonetically spell the nonsense words was correspondingly poor. Though this is not quantitative research, it does indicate a trend, linking symbol imagery with phonemic awareness and spelling ability.

Apparently, my mom wasn't really a wizard, as she often appeared so many years ago. It was really just her well developed *symbol imagery* that allowed her to rattle off the letters in a word, lightning fast. She simply saw the letters in her mind, visualized them, and then named the letters she saw, verbalized them. "T-O-M-O-*double*-R-O-W."

Tomorrow is here. Let's learn about the relationship between symbol imagery and reading/spelling, and then let's learn how to teach it. Quite a missing link, I think.

The Gestalt of Reading
& Symbol Imagery's
Emerging Role

How and where this process of symbol imagery is related to literacy development requires a gestalt analysis—big picture—look at the reading process. Rather than just leaping into the camp of one process or the other, and swinging with the pendulum to whatever theory is in vogue at the moment, we must view the reading process as an interactive whole. Years ago, I diagrammed the interaction between phonological processing, sight words, contextual fluency, and comprehension in what I called the *Reading Circles,* a Venn diagram.

The reading circles paradigm illustrates reading as an interactive process.

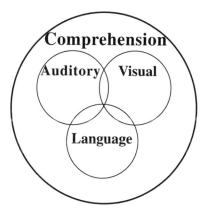

The Comprehension Circle

Though letters and words may be the parts—stars—of the cognitive universe, they are not the universe. Meaning is the universe. Reasoning. Critical thinking. Interpretation. Comprehension.

Thus, the largest circle is the universe, labeled above as the Comprehension Circle. The inner circles are subsets of this greater set; subsets that enable meaning, but do not guarantee it. Being able to comprehend requires the ability to code in two ways, as language and imagery (dual coding). Paivio (1986), "Cognition is proportional to the extent that the coding mechanisms of mental representations and language are integrated." Extracting meaning from oral language is cognition; extracting meaning from printed language (reading comprehension) is also cognition. Bell (1991), "Reading comprehension requires concept imagery—the ability to image the gestalt, *whole*."

Processing the whole eludes many people. Grasping only parts, they may recall a few details, names, dates, some emotional pieces, etc., but miss the essential idea of what they read, the gestalt. Though they might seem like good readers, may decode well, have good vocabularies, read fluently in context and pass many kinds of assessments (visual-motor tests, tests of phonemic awareness, intelligence tests), they cannot comprehend oral or written language well. They lack the ability to do the kind of reasoning and critical thinking that results from imaging the gestalt.

Having said all that, it is much easier to image the whole and get meaning from written language if print is deciphered accurately and fluently. The importance of fluent decoding to comprehension has driven professionals to disputes, debates, and frustrations. Like the blind men and the elephant, many reading professionals don't realize that the cognitive underpinnings of the decoding process (accurate phonetic processing, sight word recognition, contextual cues, and oral vocabulary) are simply parts necessary for the whole. Veterans of endless wars—here are those parts.

The Auditory Circle

The Auditory Circle represents quick, accurate phonetic processing—the ability to accurately and confidently sound out a word.

- Put all the sounds in the right place.
- Apply "phonics" to reading.
- Self-correct an error by holding and comparing what is said with what is seen.
- Have good word attack skills.

Indeed, this is a very important aspect of reading. What I could now explain to my mother is that the reason we stopped teaching phonics was that we had many children who couldn't use it. Though they could learn the sounds and letters, children often couldn't apply "phonics" to reading and spelling, "This isn't working, disregard it!" rang throughout education; so we abandoned phonics instruction and tried something else.

The reason it wasn't working was that the children who couldn't use phonics didn't have well developed phonemic awareness—the ability to perceive the identity, number, and order of sounds within words They couldn't *hear* the sounds in words. When decoding a word, they couldn't tell *if* they were right or wrong, or *where* they were right or wrong. They had weak phonological feedback, impairing their ability to self-correct, to hold and compare their response to the stimulus.

The Visual Circle

The Visual Circle represents quick, accurate sight word recognition—not spit and grunt decoding, but rapid naming of a word.

- Recognize a word quickly and accurately.
- Have a memorized sight word base.
- Not have to sound-out a word.

This is a critical aspect of reading, requiring a base of phonological processing and visual memory. Without a good sight vocabulary, individuals are left with the task of phonetically processing many, many words or guessing from context cues. Sounding-out words causes slower reading, and guessing may be inaccurate, and both can interfere with getting meaning—imagery—from print.

When instruction in phonics didn't reach enough children, reading theorists turned heavily to a *look-say* method, which basically taught memorizing of words by a flashcard approach. Unfortunately, it is difficult to memorize all the words in our language, and some individuals have a weak visual memory;

consequently, the look-say approach failed many children, just as "phonics" did. And, the cry came again, "It's not working, disregard it." Basically abandoning sight word instruction and phonics, we turned to a different approach, one with a high cost to children and society.

The Language Circle

The Language Circle represents two areas critical to reading: contextual cues and oral vocabulary.

- Use context cues, guess from context.
- Understand the meaning of words, have a well developed oral vocabulary.

When we abandoned phonics and sight word instruction, the use of contextual constraints in reading became the primary strategy for reading instruction. A psycho-linguistic guessing game was given the name *whole language* and children were taught to guess at words based on where the words were in context and what meaning was around them. Not a bad strategy *if* you can decode and get images from concepts. However, if you are a poor decoder then you may not have enough context from which to get meaning. And, if you have difficulty imaging concepts, the guessing or self-correcting from context may be just from semantic or syntactic cues, but not the gestalt or concepts the written words are transmitting.

A well developed oral vocabulary is critical to getting meaning from print, and decoding a word will have little value without an image for its meaning. Recall (imagine, one and the same) sitting at a restaurant in a France, staring at a menu with what must contain certain delicacies, placing your order by sounding out the French word(s)—then realizing that almost anything might turn up on your plate! You had no imagery/meaning to put with the word you used to order your food. Words become meaningful through imagery, and oral vocabulary is a very important part of the gestalt of reading.

Sensory-Cognitive Functions

With the circles in mind, *two primary areas of sensory-cognitive function are necessary to reading: phonemic awareness and concept imagery.* Phonemic awareness is primary to decoding and concept imagery is primary to comprehension. Weakness in either or both areas may manifest itself in reading difficulty, low self-esteem, poor expressive language, the label of dyslexia, hyperlexia, attention deficit, hyperactivity, "not motivated," or "not very bright."

Children and adults with weakness in phonemic awareness will predictably have difficulty in: 1) understanding the logic of our alphabetic system, 2) sounding out words accurately and fluently, and 3) self-correcting errors in reading and spelling. They have difficulty getting the words off the page.

Children and adults with weakness in concept imagery will predictably have difficulty in: 1) comprehending and interpreting what is read, 2) comprehending and interpreting what is heard, 3) following directions, and 4) thinking logically and critically. They have difficulty getting the meaning off the page, and understanding and interpreting oral language.

But, how does symbol imaging fit into these two areas? Here's a story that was my first clue regarding the possible split in imagery, and the relationship between symbol imagery and phonemic awareness.

Allan was a college student whose primary complaint was that he couldn't spell well. He said he got by in reading, but his spelling was weak, and in general he had to limit his writing to what he could spell rather than what he could think. His performance on the Lindamood Auditory Conceptualization (LAC) Test was weak, as was his performance on the Visual Memory for Letters subtest of the Detroit Test of Learning Aptitude (DTLA), the latter being something I didn't fit into the equation at the time. Although weakness in visual memory for letters was often parallel with weakness on the LAC Test, I didn't know how to think about it since on the surface it seemed *visual* and thus unrelated to the *auditory* task of perceiving sounds in words.

One afternoon, in a small office, just the two of us working, I tired of giving Allan nonsense and real words to spell. He was fatigued and frustrated by the process of spelling and noting irregularities. His tracking of sounds was good, though not quite automatic. I couldn't lose him in complex one syllable patterns nor in multisyllable patterns. He still had to *think* about the sounds in the words. So, I turned to a completely different task in an effort to give him a break.

"Allan, read this page for me, and tell me what you've read."

Allan read the high level passages aloud, very well, and gave me a succinct and interpretive summary. This he liked. This he could do. He looked up, pleased, only to see my puzzled look.

"How can you do that so easily? What do you *do* to help yourself comprehend?"

His reply, well known now by those of you who have read *the Visualizing and Verbalizing for Language Comprehension and Thinking* (V/V) book or studied my work on concept imagery, was a bewildered and somewhat shy, "I make movies when I read."

Ensuing discussion took place regarding this phenomenon that was new to me. He told me how he could visualize the events and the relationships and use the images for comprehension and memory. He saw the concepts in his head as he read, and he saw them rapidly, though he'd not really thought about it before I asked. It wasn't something he did consciously, it was something he did automatically—unconsciously.

Now he was puzzled. Didn't everyone visualize when they read? Was he different? Didn't I see things when I read?

Thinking of the books I read into the night as a child, *The Black Stallion, Gone with the Wind, To Kill a Mockingbird,* I could conjure up images just recalling them. Certainly I imaged when I read! We discussed this further and then my thoughts turned back to his spelling needs.

I'll use imagery to help him remember how to spell these words that are frustrating him so, and that he loses in his memory system from one day to the next. "Allan, let's see if you can visualize the letters for these words we're spelling. Can you see the letters for the word *construction*?"

Thoughtful. Very thoughtful. "No. I don't see anything."

Hmmm. How can that be? "Nothing?"

Thoughtful again. "No, nothing."

Now, I knew he knew what it meant to visualize something since he had just described his ability to image in detail. And, I knew he was trying. There were no distractions. What was the problem?

I'll try again. This time a smaller word. "How about the word *enough*?" Can you see letters for that?"

Quiet. Thoughtful again. "No. I don't see any letters."

I tried again, smaller. "How about the word *cat*? What letters do you see for that?"

"I don't see any letters, really, but I can easily see a cat. I can make it a black cat, a tiger cat, a cat sitting under the kitchen table, a white cat on a red chair, but…I'm sorry. I just can't see the letters."

Holy moly. How could that be? How could he easily and automatically see concepts, some quite intricate, demanding movement and color, action and *integration*, but not see *letters*?

I questioned him about it, and tried a few more, but clearly he couldn't easily see the letters. After he left, I went back and looked at his diagnostic testing. His oral vocabulary was very high, his oral language comprehension and ability to follow directions were also very high; his word recognition was adequate; his paragraph decoding accuracy was good, as was his reading comprehension. His math skills were good. His visual-motor skills were good. Where was he weak? There it was: LAC Test (phonemic awareness), word attack, spelling, and *visual memory for letters*.

Allan had good concept imagery, thus good comprehension and ability to follow directions, but his symbol imagery was weak, and not coincidentally, so was his phonemic awareness, spelling and word attack. Unfortunately, at that time, I was so interested in the phenomena of imagery's relationship to comprehension that I didn't pursue imagery's relationship to phonemic awareness and thus didn't fully teach Allan to spell. To my everlasting sadness, Allan's spelling improved phonetically, but did not reach the same level of confidence and accuracy that his reading reached.

But, time went on, and symbol imagery kept surfacing, pushing and struggling to emerge, refusing to be a stepchild to our other concepts. Delivering gains in word recognition and spelling every time we remembered to stress it, it finally surfaced as specific stimulation, separating itself from phonemic awareness and concept imagery. Now symbol imagery's time has come and the remainder of this book will help cement symbol imagery's place in the battlefield of reading and spelling, and teach you how to stimulate it. I can find no reason for understanding about symbol imagery, if you do not also know how to develop it. Theory without practical application, solutions, is really quite useless, but the reverse is also true. Applying specific methodology without understanding its conceptual base limits its usefulness. Instruction must be useful and meaningful, working toward a whole. Look at the problems we have created and endured in the field of reading because we have lacked an understanding of brain function and methods for implementing theory.

4

Phonemic Awareness &
Symbol Imagery: 1, 2, 3

As symbol imagery unfolds as a sensory cognitive function, we have to continue thinking from the gestalt. Phonemic awareness and symbol imagery are mates in the sensory system for language processing, specifically literacy development. Since previous chapters discussed what symbol imagery is, let's begin this chapter with understanding phonemic awareness.

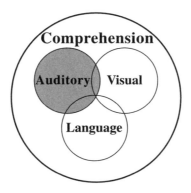

Phonemic awareness is the ability to perceive the identity, number, and order of sounds within words—the Auditory Circle. It is the ability to hear sounds in words, segment one from the other, a base for processing single syllable through multisyllable words. The latter being especially critical, as most individuals who have difficulty reading and spelling words have difficulty at the multisyllable level. Although perception for sounds in words may not be intact for single syllable words, the abilities developed in the visual and/or language circles may leap up and assist with memorization of words or use of context, respectively. While memorizing words or guessing reasonably well may support reading of easier material, weakness in phonemic awareness at the multisyllable level will interfere with accurate decoding and thus accurate comprehension.

The Role of Phonemic Awareness in Reading and Spelling

To understand the role of phonemic awareness in reading and spelling, think of the Auditory, Visual, Language, and Comprehension Circles. Phonemic awareness is the foundation of the Auditory Circle. Without the ability to perceive sounds in words, it is difficult to apply sound/letter associations to reading and spelling words; and consequently, it is difficult to understand the basis for our alphabetic reading and spelling system. A physician with severe weakness in perceiving sounds said that reading and spelling was always a mystery to him because he thought there were *thousands* of sounds in English. Why did he think that? He couldn't segment one sound from the other because the sounds in the words smooshed together to seem like one sound; thus, every word was a sound—hence thousands of sounds in English. Our sound/letter reading and spelling system was a complete mystery to him. How did he get by? For reading, he memorized words and used contextual cues to guess, but he often had to reread material to be sure he filled in the right decoding blank. He said he studied hours and hours longer than other medical students trying to figure out the medical terms. For spelling, he avoided what he could, but for the lengthy, multisyllable medical terms, he memorized the shape, how many ups and downs the words had at certain points in the overall shape. The sounds and letters, which you and I use so easily, were of no help because his sensory system couldn't process their relevancy to reading and spelling.

Intact phonemic awareness is necessary to *apply* sound/letter associations to reading a word or spelling a word, and fundamental to *self-correction*. Decoding errors, or spelling errors, are made by everyone at one time or another; *but,* if our phonemic awareness is good, we can *hold and compare* our response to the stimulus, judge our errors and make the correction. Because we can self-correct, we are *independent* readers and spellers. We don't need someone telling us that we left out an **r**, or added an **l**, or didn't process a middle syllable correctly.

Here is a phonemic awareness diagram illustrating the relationship of phonemic awareness to reading.

Johnny looks at the word stream and says "steam." If his phonemic awareness is not intact, he will need a teacher, parent, or friend to tell him that he left out the r. His sensory system won't be able to match response to stimulus and self-correct. The problem is compounded in multisyllable words, where he may look at immigration and say "imagination," and again not be able to self-correct because of weakness in phonemic awareness. Even if contextual cues could signal that "immigration" does not fit with the meaning of the sentence or paragraph, without intact phonemic awareness Johnny's primary reading strategy is to guess, again. Or he may have already made so many decoding errors that he doesn't have enough context available from which to know that meaning is interrupted, so he'll guess again—probably in error. It is certainly easier to just teach him to decode accurately in the first place!

Phonemic awareness is an essential part of the *independence* paradigm (see below). Like dominos, one processing ability spills onto the other, beginning with sensory input and ending with independence.

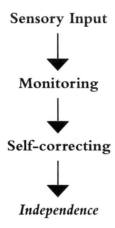

Sensory Input

⬇

Monitoring

⬇

Self-correcting

⬇

Independence

Developing phonemic awareness is imperative to reading and spelling accuracy. As the theorists have readopted it as a critical factor in reading and spelling, what may follow is a return to "phonics" instruction, with old phonics programs dusted off and new ones created. However, confusion between phonics and phonemic awareness can move us backward rather than forward. Teachers may teach phonics again, but not teach phonemic awareness. Children with weakness in perceiving sounds in words still won't be able to *apply* sound/ letters to reading and spelling. "Phonics" will be held to blame and the engines of the literacy war will roar again. So, we'll drop phonics and start something new. You and I may be gone, but our children might resurface sight word instruction as the primary strategy; then when that doesn't work along may come a grandchild of a psycho-linguist to demand that just putting good literature in the children's hands will teach them to read! We must see that reading is an integration of skills with underlying sensory cognitive processes as the foundation. Phonemic awareness is one of the basic processes and symbol imagery is a part of it.

Only recently, we learned that phonemic awareness is not just auditory, it is also articulatory. This is a relatively new concept, now becoming widely accepted. When Pat Lindamood, a speech therapist, wrote the ADD Program, she did it on the basis of instinct, background, and experience. I entered the picture when the ADD Program was being published, the LAC Test wasn't published yet, and was fortunate to be involved in one of the first pilot projects using the ADD program in a public school environment. What Pat developed was significant in three ways: 1) a test, the LAC Test, to measure what she called auditory conceptualization (phonemic awareness), 2) the use of articulatory feedback to give students a *concrete* way to perceive sounds, and 3) the use of colored blocks to apply that articulatory feedback to the development of phonemic awareness.

Prior to the LAC Test, measurements of phonemic awareness were not precise enough and educational theory got off track. Tests such as the Wepman Auditory Discrimination Test or the Rosner were measuring gross levels of auditory discrimination and thus could not demonstrate a relationship between reading and spelling. For example, on the Wepman, if an individual could say that "dag" and "mag" were different, they did well on the test. However, they may have done poorly in reading and spelling, so it appeared there wasn't a direct relationship between auditory discrimination and reading and spelling. Without evidence of a relationship and too much failure resulting from phonics instruction, we moved our focus in reading from phonetic processing to sight words and then use of context. But, it wasn't that phonemic awareness was unrelated, it was that we weren't measuring it precisely enough to show the relationship. Like early diagnosticians in neurology, who tried to make treatment decisions by using EEG's to quantify brain functions that we know now can only be demonstrated through PET scans, we were trying to make decisions about literacy without the right information. Early measurements didn't have a *hold and compare* component, where individuals had to show how and where the two patterns were different, necessary since it is hold and compare (monitoring) that we do when we self-correct. The LAC Test, which measures hold and compare processing by contrasting an old and a new pattern and asking an individual to demonstrate how and where the patterns are different, helped demonstrate the quantifiable relationship between phonemic awareness and reading and spelling words—a significant contribution to the field of literacy.

Also, what Pat knew logically was that even if individuals couldn't hear sounds, they could *feel* sounds (articulatory feedback)—another significant contribution to the field of literacy. Articulatory feedback is a critical factor in concretizing phonemes for individuals; and, that concretizing can be labeled with language, and applied to tracking sounds in syllables. Pat labeled the articulatory feedback for phonemes with language associated to the feeling. In fact, the language of the labels created an image for the feeling. Lip popper. Tongue tapper. Lip Cooler. Tongue Cooler. Without consciously intending to, Pat created a multisensory aspect of phoneme identification that went beyond articulatory and auditory sensory input and moved into the sensory input of imagery. *The language of the labels called imagery to mind,* which called kinesthetic feedback to mind, which in turn could be tracked concretely in syllables, Pat's third contribution.

In the ADD program, after the labeling of consonants and vowels, tracking is introduced. Using little colored blocks, students sequence sounds within syllables representing each phoneme with a block; they are developing their phonemic awareness with articulatory feedback. They are *feeling* the phonemes to support hearing them. For example, for a pattern such as "pim", the student places one block for each sound in the syllable and completes the tracking by saying each sound while touching the corresponding block. Saying and touching the blocks, sensory input comes from the student's mouth. He or she is *feeling* it, not hearing it. Asked to change "pim" to "fim", the student changes the block representing the /p/ and labels the change by saying "the lip popper went out and the lip cooler came in." The labels reinforce the articulatory feedback, again the student is feeling the changes, not hearing them. The stimulation purposely begins with feeling.

At the Lindamood-Bell Center, we took hundreds of students through the ADD program's tracking of sounds through articulatory feedback; and, no matter the age, given enough time, their ability to track the sounds through the use of articulatory feedback improved. But, we often noted that the process could be frustratingly slow to stabilize for some students. The more severe the weakness the more difficulty the students had in feeling the sounds; and the more difficulty they had reaching stability and the automaticity of rapid processing. There were days when their processing seemed to be established, then days when it seemed to vanish. Sitting across from a child struggling with the blocks or an adult perspiring with intensity, I used to think that there must be a faster way to stabilize their phonological processing. Day after day, week after week, month after month, year after year, until finally it occurred to me that a piece might be missing.

Around this time, I also noted we consistently reached a point during the tracking aspect of ADD when our students didn't need to label the changes anymore; labeling slowed them down. They didn't need to verify phonemes with their mouth; their processing was becoming automatic. I began to ask the question that if they weren't verifying with their mouth, what were they using to recognize and verify changes so rapidly? Watching and analyzing, my experience with Allan (who could image concepts but not words) and TO–M–O–R–R–O–W crept through the mist into my consciousness—and symbol imagery was born.

Articulatory Blocks vs. Auditory Blocks

The students I saw who had to struggle to make the changes, though accurate, were vastly different that those who could make the changes automatically. These two types of processing blocks began to be labeled in my clinical notes. I labeled them: articulatory blocks and auditory blocks.

Articulatory blocks were when the student still needed to say the sound and touch the block (say and touch) for the old and new pattern. For example, Johnny had to *feel* the changes because he couldn't hear the changes. So he carefully said each sound as he touched each block, "*fresp*" to "*flesp*." He relied on feedback from his mouth, just as we had so carefully taught him to do. But, he had difficulty getting beyond it, requiring lots of practice, tons of blocks that he began to hate and despise. More importantly, he was having trouble self-correcting, because if he made an error, he had to check his mouth for feedback, a *slow* process. Worse, when he was reading in context and made a decoding error, in order to self-correct he had to go back to his mouth and check every sound he said against every sound he saw. Slow, painfully slow, and ultimately, too slow for Johnny; so in contextual reading he reverted back to a guessing strategy and his clinicians or teachers pulled their hair out in frustration. Puzzled, they agonized, "Why isn't Johnny *using* his new skills? Why is he still guessing when he reads, why doesn't he sound out words?"

Like we do, Johnny read for meaning, but it took him too long to check every word by matching sounds to articulatory feelings. So in an effort to read fluently and gather meaning, he didn't always have the patience to take the time to slowly match response to stimulus. Thus, he did it some of the time, but not all the time. What he needed was automaticity. Quick, rapid processing. The answer to the Johnny-puzzle was that his new skills had not yet reached a level of automaticity rapid enough for him to apply them to the integration needed for reading in context.

And, that automaticity is what we noted as *auditory blocks*. When our clinical notes began to say, "the blocks are becoming auditory," it was because Charlie didn't have to say and touch and feel the sounds anymore. He could *hear* them. As it turned out, he could also *see* them. When the two patterns were said to him, he could respond rapidly by just moving the appropriate block. "If that says *glisp*, show me *glips*." He quickly shifted the last two blocks—not checking his mouth. Rapid responses. Automaticity. Very soon I began to realize that what was really happening was that the two patterns were *held and compared by a strengthened auditory system that enabled imaging the letters.* Consistency began to occur, stabilization, quick changes, just like individuals who didn't have weakness in phonemic awareness. We had taken a student who couldn't perceive sounds in words and changed him into a student with no difficulty. Why couldn't I do that for everyone? What was it that Charlie was doing that was different from what he did before intervention? What was it that led to this automaticity? And, if there was something, couldn't it be developed *sooner*, and stability developed more quickly?

In attempting to answer these questions, I observed that Charlie, unlike Johnny, was starting to spontaneously say the letter names when he made the change. He spontaneously dropped the labeling, which meant he did not have to feel the sounds anymore, and instead said letter names. Other students who reached the point of auditory blocks also did the same thing, giving letters not labels. A threshold point was evident, a movement from one state to the other, leading to automaticity. Some students reached that point without direct stimulation, while others never seemed to reach it. Of great to concern to me at the time was that I sometimes had clinicians who were afraid to let a student drop the labeling for fear it meant the ADD Program wasn't being implemented accurately. But, what became more and more evident was that *seeing* the changes led to rapid processing; symbol imagery, spelling bees, a mother spewing out letters seemingly without thought, a young man very disabled in spelling who couldn't spew or see any letters, all came to mind.

Up the Sensory System: One, Two, Three

The sensory system works as a unit, a whole, especially for the development of what we have labeled phonemic awareness. We walk up and down the sensory system as we need to, beginning with feeling in the mouth (where sounds are created), moving to auditory, and then landing in symbol imagery. One, two, three. If there is weakness in perceiving sounds within words, stimulating kinesthetic, articulatory, feedback may be the first step, but symbol imagery is the last step.

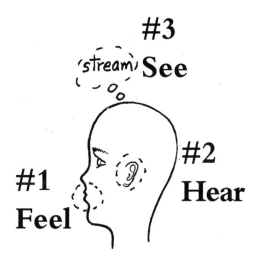

The importance of moving up from articulatory/auditory processing to symbol imagery can't be emphasized enough. The point of decoding is to extract meaning from print which requires fluency, processing speed and efficiency of effort. Verifying decoding attempts through articulatory feedback requires time, modest though it may be, but time nonetheless; imaging the letters on the other hand is a rapid process. Symbol imagery yields automaticity for the skills of the Auditory Circle.

For example, in the Auditory Circle, developing phonemic awareness for word attack requires applying sound/letter correspondence to decoding the word (sounding it out), monitoring that processing for accuracy, and then self-correcting if there is an error when response to stimulus doesn't match—"steam" for *stream*. If ability in symbol imagery has been developed, by moving up the sensory system, then the matching process is rapid—consisting of matching (holding and comparing) letters to letters—what was *seen* in both cases. For example, Charlie might look at *stream* and say "steam," and *see* that he left out the **r** by comparing the letters he imaged with the letters he saw on the page. He compares what was *seen—imagery to print*—rather than comparing what was felt or heard with print, a more time consuming act.

The automaticity of symbol imagery allows for rapid processing and quick self-correction. Rather than slowly having to match each sound with what is heard or felt, *the matching is between imaged letters to print*. Rapid processing transfers over to spontaneous self-correction in context; and because the processing is not laborious and time consuming, an individual's reading fluency is maintained and guessing is reduced.

So symbol imagery is an essential part of phonemic awareness. It is, at least, the end result of phonemic awareness. But *perhaps symbol imagery is phonemic awareness.* Despite the fact that the *language* we use to describe decoding and encoding conjures up images of sound (*phonemic* awareness, *phonological* processing, *auditory* discrimination, etc.), perhaps symbol imagery is phonological processing in its final resting place. Or perhaps they are separate functions and symbol imagery only assists in the integrated process that results in automaticity in reading and spelling. In reality, does it matter what name we give it as long as we reach the goal of automaticity in processing sounds and letters?

Thinking phonemic awareness is related to imagery is no more astounding than thinking phonemic awareness is related to articulatory feedback. *The sensory system was created to integrate sensory information—articulatory, auditory, imagery—in an ingenious fashion of togetherness.*

Word Recognition
Needs Symbol Imagery

One of the war-cries on the battle field of literacy is that developing word attack skills does not necessarily transfer to good word recognition, fluent contextual reading, or reading comprehension. While this is true, word attack is a critical part of the reading process, not the whole but an essential part; and another essential part is *instant word recognition*. Often assumed and rarely given enough attention, the skills of the Visual Circle are just as necessary for fluent reading as phonetic processing.

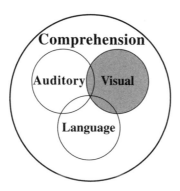

The Visual Circle: A Problem Identified and Solved

The Visual Circle represents a memorized sight vocabulary—an efficient way to process those written words, that orthography, occuring with enormous frequency or made up of letter combinations that defy standard word attack strategies. Its development depends on two foundational processes: phonemic awareness and symbol imagery. Phonemic awareness is part of the foundation of sight vocabulary skills, enabling self-correction and the processing of sounds and letters. In fact, without phonemic awareness and word attack skills, individuals would need to guess at or memorize nearly every word they encountered. Automaticity in phonemic awareness and confident word attack skills support the development of a sight vocabulary, but don't guarantee it.

Perhaps some of you have experienced the frustration of teaching a phonetic processing approach, seeing students somewhat able to sound-out unfamiliar words, but not seeing those word attack skills easily transfer to the development of sight words or accurate, fluent decoding in context or reading comprehension. At Lindamood-Bell Centers, before we were aware of the importance of stimulating symbol imagery, we had students who would make significant gains in word attack, years of improvement, but not achieve the same high level of gains in word recognition or paragraph reading. The problem was twofold: 1) we spent too long developing phonetic processing, too much play in the auditory camp that still didn't reach a level of automaticity in processing, and 2) we had not developed the sensory-cognitive base underlying the ability to memorize words. In both cases, the inclusion of symbol imagery to our instructional paradigm changed the results.

Here is an example. Marcus was a fifth grade boy, with average intelligence, who came to us with a painful history. Early on in school he had difficulty responding to reading instruction, and was finally retained in second grade. By third grade, he still hadn't learned to read and was further behind. Continuing to have difficulty learning to read in school, even in special education classes, he was taken to private tutoring that used a highly respected approach to reading instruction. Very minimal progress. Marcus knew some sounds and letters, and knew he was supposed to apply them to the words on the page, but he just couldn't do it consistently. With high-average oral vocabulary, Marcus's potential was being wasted and he was developing serious self-image problems.

By fifth grade, when Marcus was sent to us he had become a moderate behavior problem in that his teachers felt he wasn't motivated and tended to talk to the other students during "seat work." Our diagnostic testing revealed a severe weakness in phonemic awareness (the LAC Test), word attack skills at the *first grade level*, word recognition at the *first grade level*, and paragraph decoding at the *first grade level*, spelling at the *first grade level*, very weak reading comprehension, severe weakness in visual memory for letters, and high-average oral vocabulary.

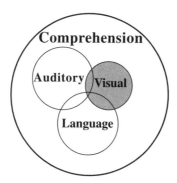

Using the ADD program, Marcus responded to the stimulation of articulatory feedback and began to track sounds in words and apply that tracking to reading and spelling both nonsense and "play-fair" real words. For the first time, he began to understand the logic of our alphabetic system. But, when we turned to teaching sight words, we came up against a serious memory problem. He could look at the word *know* and recognize it one moment but not the next, often just seconds later. Phonetic processing was available to him now, but was still very slow. He couldn't learn sight words easily and was frustrated with how often he had to go over them in order to remember them, and just when he thought he had some, when we checked a week later, they were gone. He couldn't just spit them out. He had to go back and laboriously try to sound them out; and the ones that didn't play fair drove him crazy. In context and out, guessing returned, as Marcus tried to make the word match his good oral vocabulary, his lexicon.

We did a retest after approximately three to four months of intensive treatment. His word attack had improved to the sixth grade level, and his word recognition and paragraph reading to the third grade level. Significant gains after years of failure; but, he was still not able to function well in school. His contextual reading was very slow, he frequently guessed instead of processing, and his teacher said that although he had made progress, he was still quite far behind. His spelling was fairly phonetic, but not accurate, and he was doing poorly on spelling tests in school because he couldn't memorize the words. Or if he memorized some of them for the test, he couldn't spell them two days later when writing a story or paragraph; much frustration prevailed in all camps, Marcus' in particular.

The retest showed two very illuminating facts hindering Marcus's progress. Fact one: although he scored significantly higher in phonemic awareness, he was *slow* to make the changes on the LAC Test. Fact two: his visual memory for letters had not improved. For example, when a stimulus card consisting of a random selection of consonant letters was held up for a few seconds and then taken away, Marcus still had much difficulty remembering and saying what he saw. When it was a card with two letters, he could remember and say them. When it was a card with three letters, he could still remember and say them. When it was a card with four letters, he started having difficulty remembering and saying them. But, when it was a card with five letters, he couldn't perform. No wonder he couldn't learn sight words! He couldn't remember them. He didn't have a way in his sensory system to hold them. He didn't have good symbol imagery, or what has commonly been referred to as visual memory for letters.

Marcus needed symbol imagery to: 1) improve his automaticity in phonological processing, to hasten his word attack skills and ability to self-correct, 2) improve his ability to remember sequences of letters, to develop his sight word recognition, 3) improve his fluency in contextual reading (because his phonetic processing would be rapid and his sight words would be developed) and 4) improve his ability to remember words for spelling.

We started symbol imagery with Marcus, and as would be expected, it was very difficult for him to visualize letters. But, within a few weeks, he could see letters and write them in the air, say the letters backwards, identify a certain letter within the stream of letters he was holding in his imagery, decode from his imaged patterns, correct my miscalling from the imaged patterns, and make automatic changes in blocks. Self-correction in reading became much quicker because his sensory system *saw* his error from the imaged hold-and-compared pattern; and he could *remember* his sight words. Not surprisingly, at the final retest 1) his visual memory for letters had improved significantly, 2) his LAC Test responses were automatic, 3) his word attack processing was quick and accurate, and he gained a few more years, 4) his word recognition gained three years, a result of rapid phonetic processing and an expanded base of sight words, and 5) his paragraph reading gained three years from that same rapid phonetic processing and expanded base of sight words integrating with his good vocabulary and language comprehension. The result of all this was the best gain; Marcus felt he had conquered learning to read and spell. He felt good about himself, and as I looked at him I knew he would have to face more of life's challenges, as do we all, but at least no longer would his have to be related to reading, spelling, and learning.

Imagery and memory have a documented relationship, and the ability to image symbols (letters) is a necessary function underlying the acquisition of sight words.

Contextual Reading:
an Act of Integration

Decoding in context for meaning is the real world of reading, and an act of integration, using the processes already discussed. *Contextual reading requires both the Auditory and Visual Circle to be in tact, but also concept imagery to assist with meaning and contextual hypothesizing.* When the Auditory Circle is fully functioning, quick accurate word attack and self-correction are available processes for reading in context. Integrating these two develops the Language Circle of contextual fluency.

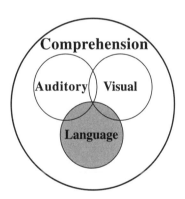

When we read a sentence, paragraph, or page, we are interacting with print in numerous and significant ways. We are using imagery for meaning, and checking that imagery to see that what we decode makes sense. We are using phonological processing and symbol imagery for self-correcting. We are using a memorized sight word base to provide fluent, rapid decoding. But, what happens when we make an error (which we all do on occasion)? If we read the sentence, *the tree drips sap from its trunk* as "the tree *dips* sap from its trunk," first imagery/meaning triggers the correction and the need to reread or check. Then phonological processing and symbol imagery kick in and we quickly correct the error. Efficient reading is reading primarily for meaning and not reading primarily to match sounds and letters—decodimg. While the matching of sounds and letters is critical to getting the meaning, it is not meaning, and it is not what we instinctively read to achieve. And, this is what started the debate in literacy about *surface structure vs. deep structure*, attention to decoding words (the surface: integrating phonological processing and symbol imagery) vs. attention to meaning (deep structure: integrating vocabulary and concept imagery). But, it is not an either/or issue; it is not a surface structure or deep structure issue. It is an integration of processes, and *integration can only occur if the underlying sensory-cognitive functions are intact*. Thus, developing phonemic awareness and symbol imagery for the Auditory and Visual Circles is imperative for word processing, as is developing concept imagery for integration with vocabulary.

The Language Circle requires good phonological processing and symbol imagery, a well developed sight vocabulary, and a well developed oral vocabulary, but it also needs development as a stand alone entity in the reading process. Once the foundational skills are established, students need practice, *experience*, flowing across the page from word to word, imaging, anticipating, self-correcting, attending to print while integrating it with imagery/meaning. They need practice with good literature to enhance their enjoyment, improve their contextual reading skills, improve their ability to image concepts, think, interpret, reason, and improve their oral vocabulary and expressive language.

We need to keep in mind that while the Auditory and Visual Circles are a critical part of the literacy game, they are not the whole game. The game is processing written language with the same ease and fluency that we process oral language. That kind of ease requires an integration of word attack, word recognition, contextual reading, accurate spelling, oral vocabulary, and language comprehension and interpretation—skills whose foundations stem from our sensory-cognitive systems.

7

Hav and Opertunity:
Spelling & Symbol Imagery

Spelling is a partner to reading and a significant other to expressive written language. Long misunderstood, often hated, given too little attention in the field of literacy, and in danger of dismissal because of computer spell-checkers, spelling is a compilation of the stars in the Universe.

As with reading, spelling is an integration of sensory-cognitive functions, but quite less complicated than reading. Over the years of teaching children and adults to spell accurately, two *primary* functions have sifted through the haze: Auditory and Visual, phonemic awareness and symbol imagery, respectively. This is not to say that understanding the morphological (meaning) aspect of words, use of roots, syntactic patterns for tenses, and the vast amount of spelling rules, aren't important helpers in spelling. But, by developing phonemic awareness and symbol imagery, children and adults have the necessary underpinnings, basic functions, to learn to spell.

Clearly, phonemic awareness is critical to spelling. It is imperative to be able to perceive the sounds in words in order to spell. Without this ability, spelling has to be completely memorized, either by rules or imagery for the word pattern. Here is a good place to recall the neurologist that we met in chapter four, who thought every word was a sound because he couldn't segment one sound from the other in syllables. Remember, he spelled by the up and down of the medical words, and couldn't perceive the sounds well enough to get past the first sound in order to use a dictionary? In fact, as a child I can remember children in my one room school asking the teacher for help to spell a word and having her respond, "Look it up in the dictionary." I remember the configuration of the classroom, the windows placed so I could look on the mountains in rural California, and the face of one of my classmates having difficulty learning to read—and who also couldn't spell. He would reluctantly get the dictionary out of his desk and start going through page after page.

When I went over to help him, he would be searching somewhere completely unreasonable. He often didn't know where to go after the first letter. His face was fraught with frustration. He hated school. He hated spelling. He was one of the behavior problems in the tiny school of sixteen children.

I, on the other hand, had been dealt a genetic hand that enabled me to love spelling. Little Nanci did get A's on all spelling tests, and hated to have to write the words ten times to study them, thinking it was a useless exercise, since she could already spell them. I remember, being alone in my grade in that white and green school house, with the green chalk board at the front of the room, and the supply room in the back where I spent a lot of time because it had the extra reading books and workbooks that I was allowed to do. One day, released from the supply room, I looked up at the board and saw the word *answer*. Hmmm. My little mind wondered. Why does that word have a **w** in it? I don't hear a /w/.

It was good phonemic awareness that allowed me to note the irregularity in the word, just as it was good phonemic awareness that allowed my son, Rhett, to come running into the kitchen when he was in first or second grade and say to me, "Mom, what is a s*w*ord?" Curiosity all over his face, eyes glittering, he eagerly waited my response.

Chuckling, I said, "It's a sord, Rhett. A sord."

Puzzled but accepting, he thought for a moment, thanked me, and then left the room. But, he didn't get far before he turned and came back into the kitchen.

Smiling, with a gleam in his eye, he said, "Oh, sort of like a *knife*, huh," and, away he went. Spelling was always as easy as breathing for Rhett. One, two, three. He was just in step with anything to do with literacy, and though he would have other challenges in life, reading, spelling, and academics, were not a part of them.

Phonemic awareness needs to be developed from one syllable to multisyllables. If only developed at the one syllable level, students will very likely add, omit, or substitute sounds in the interior syllables. "Equetment" for *equipment*. "Insitute" for *institute*.

Despite the importance of phonemic awareness and the teaching of phonetic processing as a precursor to spelling accuracy, there is a fairly common complaint among people who instruct in phonetic processing—their own spelling becomes poor! Often, teachers and therapists say that after teaching phonics they can't spell anymore. This is a reality caused by too much emphasis on the phonological aspect of reading, interrupting the *visual* patterns, the symbol imagery, of words stored in the brain.

Here is my experience with this phenomena. One hectic morning, in the daily saga of getting three children to school and myself to the clinic, I experienced a stunning loss in my ability to spell. Through the questions and answers about lunches, shoes tied, milk money, homework, and the pushing and shoving of two loving brothers mingled with teasing a younger sister, I was attempting to leave a note for the plumber. Grabbing paper and a pen, I sat down to write him a quick note about the upstairs *fosset*. That didn't look right. *Fosset.* Sounds are in the right place, maybe it has an **i** instead of an **e**. *Fossit.* No. That doesn't look right either. I stared and stared in disbelief. I can spell this word, for heavens sake. No, it is not a **ph** in the beginning. That certainly doesn't look right. F…O…S…E…T. Is there some spelling rule I should know here? No, "**i** before **e**" can't apply. OK. I'll look it up. I can't leave a note with a misspelled word for the plumber, especially such an easy word as fossett! Going to the dictionary, children everywhere, I looked under **f - o**. Not there. Then I searched my phonological universe for what else it could be. Well, it could be the letter **a**, or **au**. Flipping the pages, children's conversation behind me, around me, in front of me, I went to **f-a.** Ah-hah, instantly my spelling gnome returned to me and I could spell the word without hesitation—*faucet*. No worries. The word was back in my head and of course it was accurate. Faucet. Perfectly phonetic, but then that really wasn't the problem in the first place. The problem was that I had lost the visual pattern. I couldn't see it anymore, and when I went back to the fail safe system of phonology or rules, it didn't help since there were a number of ways the word could be spelled phonetically: fausut, faucit, fausit, phausit, phauset, faucett, faucitt, and even fosset since we don't distinguish the /o/ from /au/ as distinctly as we should.

Symbol imagery is visual memory for letters, seeing letters in your mind's eye; however, unless directly stimulated, it may not occur spontaneously for children and adults, and what's more, it will be interrupted with instruction in only the phonetic aspect of words. Often, teaching a phonetic strategy results in gains in phonetic representations but not spelling accuracy. For example, at Lindamood-Bell, before we started including symbol imagery stimulation in our instruction, we always had significantly higher gains in word attack and decoding than spelling. Though spelling would become "more phonetically accurate," students were still doing poorly on spelling tests and in paragraph writing, where their spelling accuracy was often very poor. Although it is quite significant to improve the spelling representation of the word *opportunity* from "optrnity" to "opertunity," it is still not accurate.

It is common to teach spelling accuracy in a variety of means, including rules, word meanings, and roots, but until the underlying sensory-cognitive skills of phonemic awareness and symbol imagery are developed, those methods may not produce in the desired result. Think of this. Do you spell by recalling rules? Every time you write a word do you have to consciously remember spelling rules? It is very likely that you do not, but you may refer to them for verification of a word. Spelling is primarily an integration of phonetic processing and symbol imagery, a comparison of auditory and visual—the reason we sometimes write a word a couple of ways to see if it *looks* right.

Enough for now, I have to go and fix a dripping phaucit, er...fossit...faucit...faucett...where is that spelling gnome when you need him.

The Process

The Steps of Seeing Stars

of Seeing Stars

1. Climate

2. Imaging Letters

3. Imaging Syllable Cards

4. Imaging Syllables: Syllable Board

5. Imaging Syllables: Air-Write *with* Chain

6. Imaging Syllables: Air-Write *without* Chain

7. Imaging Sight Words

8. Imaging Spelling

9. Imaging, Reading and Spelling Two Syllables

10. Imaging, Reading and Spelling Three Syllables

11. Contextual Integration

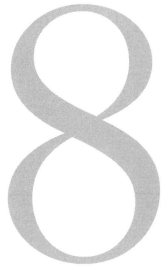

Buzz & a Guide

This chapter is a guide for some of the critical pieces of this manual—parts to help you visualize and understand the whole.

Buzz:

Buzz is a fifth grader who you will follow through each step of *Seeing Stars* to help you image the lessons, and make the stimulation real. Visualize him as shy, dark complexioned, with a buzz hair cut. Though he has learned his sounds and letters, and is doing so-so in a popular "phonics" program, he is sounding out each word in a spit-and-grunt manner, has had much difficulty learning sight words, and spells some-what phonetically. He has been retained once, exposed to numerous reading programs, and placed in special education.

Bright and scared, he is a fallen goose and I'm going down to get him...and, I'll stay until he can get back in the V formation.

Sample Lessons:

Each step has Sample Lessons presenting the teacher-student interaction; and each lesson has three parts: 1) The Set, setting the task, 2) Lesson, the interactive lesson, and 3) Lesson Summary, a short, itemized summary.

Deciphering the Code:

Here is the code for reading and relating to the sample lesson dialogue:
  • Bold capital letters refer to the letter name: **A**, **B**, **C**, **D**, **E**, etc.
  • A letter between a slash refers to the letter sound: /a/ like in at, /b/ like in bat.

- A vowel says its name when followed by the letter e: /ae/ like in ate.
- Italicized words refer to the stimulus word, many are nonsense words: *fip, ploist,* etc.

Nonsense Words:

Nonsense words are used to develop imagery for sequencing sounds in syllables; similar to real word patterns in English, examples are included in the Appendix. Though nonsense words are used, the stimulation moves between nonsense and real words, enhancing both phonetic processing and visual memory.

Chains for Hold and Compare:

Independence in reading and spelling is the goal; however, independence requires a domino reaction in the sensory system: sensory input-to monitoring-to self-correction-to independence. The sensory input domino of imaging spills onto the monitoring domino of comparing response to the stimulus. Monitoring is the ability to hold and compare...holding a response and comparing it to a stimulus. Chains of syllables, where only one letter changes at a time, develop the sensory input of imagery for holding and comparing response to stimulus. Simple and complex chains are included in the Appendix.

Irregularities and Symbol Imagery:

Throughout the *Seeing Stars* program, students are exposed to regularly irregular spelling patterns in English such as: ai, ea, oa, tch, dge, etc. A list of common spelling patterns is included in the Appendix as a reference. Only a few rules are included because we don't learn to read and spell by memorizing lots of rules. We learn to read and spell by integrating phonetic processing, with symbol imagery, with sight words, with context, with comprehension...and a few rules when our phonetic processing and/or visual memory gnomes fail us.

Symbol Imagery Exercises:

As students are moved from simple to complex syllables and into multisyllable patterns, there are four primary exercises for developing symbol imagery:

- DECODE: Student reads the syllable from the imaged pattern (memory).
- IDENTIFY: Student identifies a specific letter from the imaged pattern.
- BACKWARDS: Student says the letters backwards from the imaged pattern.
- MANIPULATE: Student reads the syllable from imagery, after letters are manipulated.

Error Handling: Responding to the Response

In a questioning, interactive program such as *Seeing Stars*, errors are handled in a positive, specific manner that continues to develop sensory-cognitive processing. A Socratic learning environment requires the teacher to ask questions, asking for thinking and a verbal or written representation of that thinking...a response requested from the learner. In order to stimulate more thinking and learning, the teacher must respond to the response.

When a student is asked to produce a response, the interaction must start from the produced response...and come in on a positive. For example, if I ask what letters Buzz sees for the card **ap** and he says, "an **A** and a **T**." I must meet him where he is, by saying, "There was an **A**, if it was an **A** and a **T** it would look like this, writing out **at**." Acknowledging the positive part of his response, I met him where he was; now, helping him compare his response to the stimulus, I hold up the **ap** card. "Is that what you saw when I showed you this card?"

Practice and Pacing:

Each chapter has a Practice and Pacing section, and while each step might be slightly different to practice and pace, there are basic concepts to note throughout the program: 1) lesson energy, 2) task levels, 3) overlapping of steps, and 4) self-correction and automaticity.

Summary Pages for Each Step:

A Summary Page at the end of each chapter succinctly summarizes the salient points of each *Seeing Stars* step. First a part of the *Visualizing and Verbalizing for Language Comprehension and Thinking* (V/V) book, the Summary Pages received rave reviews. Also included in the Appendix, the Summary Pages are together so you can more easily implement the program.

Small Group and Classroom Instruction:

The steps of *Seeing Stars* do not have to be modified for group instruction, no matter the size of the group. Each Summary Page gives specific suggestions for group practice at a given step. It is simple and fun to do all of these activities with groups. No worries.

Reading:

Most references to "reading" in this book refers to reading in context for *meaning*, not decoding, word attack, or word recognition. Those terms refer to reading words but not reading in context and comprehending. There has been confusion between teaching decoding and teaching reading; just as there has been confusion between teaching phonics and teaching phonemic awareness. Words are critical parts of the reading whole.

The Story of the Goose:

The Story of the Goose is the last chapter of *Seeing Stars*; and since laced throughout, this is a book where you probably *should* read the last chapter first! Geese fly in a V formation for a reason; bright and loyal, nurturing and smart, their story is worth reading.

The Climate:
A Short Why and What

Anything being asked of a student requires an explanation of *what* and *why*, setting an emotional tone for positive interaction. Sitting here, gazing out at my courtyard, I'm harkened back once again to a little Nanci and another lesson. I remember that my mother was often upset with one of her friends who would *tell* her daughter to do something, but not explain *why*. Mother very often said, "Children should be told a reason for doing something, then they will do it more willingly."

I'm not exactly sure that my mother's explanations worked all the time in getting me to do something, but I do remember that I would rather do the task than listen to a lengthy discussion; and, for sure, I would rather correct my behavior than be "talked to!"

So, two lessons here. One, it is important for students to know why they are going to do something with you, to know the reason, bringing an emotional commitment to learning. Two, it is important to make the explanation short and sweet. Make the point. Give the big picture, the reason, and then do it.

With reason and brevity in mind, here is the Climate for introducing *Seeing Stars*.

SAMPLE LESSON

Setting the Climate

Nanci: *"I'm going to teach you to see letters in your imagination, your mind's eye. That will help you remember letters when you read and spell like for the word 'S-E-E.' Here is a picture to help you think about that."*

59

Buzz: "OK." (Wee voice.)

Nanci: *"It's that simple, you'll learn to picture the letters in your mind and that will help you read and spell better. Try it. Close your eyes and see the letters for your name. Now write your name in the air, and say the letters as you write."*

Buzz: "Hmmm. B–U–Z–Z." (A small voice and hand tentatively says and writes the letters of his name.)

Nanci: *"Right. Letters are like the stars in the sky, parts of a whole thing called the universe. Letters are the parts of the words that we need to see."*

Buzz: (Silently watching me, eyes squinting a little...)

Nanci: *"Using your imagination for letters will help you learn to read and spell better. Really!"*

I have presented longer and shorter climates over the years, to individual children or adults, whole classes of students, and workshops of professionals. Occasionally, a professional is convinced she (or he) can't see letters, though seeming to understand what is meant by imagery. Presenting her with a longer more verbose climate explaining imagery won't teach her to visualize the letters...that will take specific stimulation. So don't get off the track and into a lengthy explanation or exchange. If someone is very vocal about not being able to see the letters, acknowledge that it may be difficult...but that's why you're doing this program. Begin the steps. Discussing a problem won't develop sensory-cognitive processing.

Summary:
Step 1

The Climate

> **Goal:** To briefly explain to the student(s) *what* and *why*.

1. "I'm going to teach you to see letters in your imagination."

2. "It will help you read and spell words better."

3. "Here's how you can picture that."

4. Diagram a head with imagery for letters.

10 Imaging Letters

Symbol imagery stimulation begins with the smallest unit to visualize—one letter. This is a simple but necessary step, helping lay the base for imaging letters in syllables. Because *Seeing Stars* can be integrated with phonics programs, the imagery of a letter symbol should be associated with the sound of the letter. The final goal for the student is to be able to say the sound as well as the letter name, and image and write it in the air.

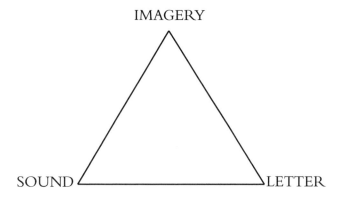

There are two steps to letter imagery: 1) *see and image,* the student sees a card with a letter on it and then images and writes, and 2) *hear and image,* the student hears a sound and then images and writes. The first one is very important for young children or those individuals who have a severe amount of difficulty visualizing letters.

The following is a sample lesson with Buzz, who has just had the climate presented to him and is reluctantly cooperating. Rather beat up by his school experience, especially in learning to read and spell, he seems to be saying this is the last time.

I've come out of the V formation and am on the ground with him.

SAMPLE LESSON

Image a Letter from a Card

The Set

Nanci: *"I'm going to show you a letter and after I take it away I want you to write it in the air and tell me the sound and letter name. This is the first step in helping your brain learn to visualize letters."* (Refer to visualize, image, or picture letters, depending on the vocabulary level of your student.)

Buzz: "OK..."

Lesson

Nanci: *"Say and write in the air what letter you see."* (I hold up a card with the letter **K** on it, then take it away.)

Buzz: "/k/, **K**." (Buzz writes the letter **K** in the air *as* he says the sound and name.)

Lesson Summary:
Image a Letter from a Card

- Teacher shows the letter card for two to three seconds.
- Student(s) sees, says, and writes in the air, giving sound and/or letter.
- Saying and air-writing should be done simultaneously.
- Student(s) air-writes in *lower case letters.*
- Student(s) air-writes *large enough* to see a "shadow" effect.
- Digraphs—sh, ch, th, wh, etc.—are considered a single unit (one sound) and included in single letter stimulation.

If you are working with kindergarten, first grade, or students that have not yet learned letter shapes and names, this is a good method for teaching the alphabet. Since Buzz does know the alphabet and has been easily able to do the step within a few moments, I move him to the next step of hearing a letter sound or name to be imaged and written in the air.

Here is Buzz moving into hearing either a letter or sound, retrieving an image for it, then saying the sound and writing it in the air.

SAMPLE LESSON

Image a letter without a Card

The Set

Nanci: *"I'm going to say a sound or a letter to you and I want you to say the sound and write it in the air. Just like you did when I showed you a letter on a card."*

Buzz: "OK. Do I write it in the air just like before, not on paper?"

Lesson

Nanci: *"Yup. Write in lower case, not gigantic, but not teeny. Try to see it in your imagination before you write it. Here is the sound: /f/."*

Buzz: **"F"** (Saying the sound, Buzz writes the letter **F** in the air.)

Nanci: *"What is the letter name for that?"*

Buzz: **"F."**

Lesson Summary:
Image a letter without a Card

- Teacher says a sound or letter.

- Student(s) says and writes in the air, gives sound and/or letter.

- Saying and air-writing are done simultaneously.

- Student(s) air-writes in *lower case letters.*

- Student(s) air-writes *large enough* to see a "shadow" effect.

How to Write in the Air

How the student writes the letters in the air is an important aspect of *Seeing Stars*. First, writing the letters should be lower case because that is the form in which written language is primarily seen. It is not often that we read capital letters or read cursive writing, thus it is not likely that we store images of words in that form, and the reverse is true. Since we normally see words in lower case, it is very likely that we store them in that form.

Second, the writing must not be too large or too small, both being equally unhelpful. Too large means the imagery may not fit on the student's internal screen, and too small or tumbling on top of one another means that the shadow effect may not be seen. The shadow effect is just what it seems, the writing leaves a shadow or ghostliness that may aid imagery.

Third, it seems preferable that the letter(s) be written *up* in the air. Though writing on a table may be effective, experience in developing symbol imagery indicates that having students write *up* is initially more productive.

How to Incorporate into the ADD Program

If using the Lindamood® ADD Program, articulatory feedback is being stimulated and given labels to describe the motor aspect of speech. Integrating symbol imagery into the ADD Program is simple: once students can *feel and label* the sound, have them *image* the letter(s).

The issue here is not to introduce symbol imagery until you are certain students have good articulatory feedback and can easily give the appropriate *label* for a sound. Move up the sensory system one, two, three: articulatory, auditory, symbol imagery. Symbol imagery will ultimately help students move more quickly through the ADD Program, and it is important to introduce it during this low level task.

The following is a demonstration lesson on how to incorporate the ADD Program labels into the symbol imagery stimulation.

SAMPLE LESSON

Imaging Letters using ADD Program Labels

with a visual stimulus—

Nanci: *"I'm going to show you a letter, tell me it's sound and label, and after I take it away, write it in the air and tell me the letter name."*

Buzz: "Like those lip poppers and things?"

Nanci: *"Right. Here we go. What is the sound and label for this letter? (I hold up the letter card with the letter **S**.)*

Buzz: "/s/, skinny air." (He writes in the air as he says the sound and label.)

without a visual stimulus—

Nanci: *"I'm going to say a sound. I want you to say the sound and the label, and write it in the air…/t/."*

Buzz: *"/t/, tip tapper."* (He writes in the air as he says the sound and label.)

How to Incorporate into Any Phonics Program

Seeing Stars can be incorporated into any phonics program, no matter what structure a specific program uses. For example, if it is the *Orton-Gillingham (OG)* Program, students can use symbol imagery as they are learning the sounds and letters. If it is the *Slingerland* Program, imagery can be discussed and stimulated as the students are saying and writing in the air. Inclusion into existing phonics programs requires very little change—just add the imagery aspect to teach sounds and letters.

Imaging in Color

At this level it is good to occasionally have the students visualize the letters in different colors. Instead of imaging black letters on a white screen, try black letters on a yellow screen, or ask students to see red letters, then green letters, then purple, etc. Some students may have to work at this, and others will do it readily as their sensory system is stimulated by the sessions. How important this is to the imaging process of the brain is not known at this time, but individuals that image with ease also see colors and movement with ease. And, the reverse is true. Individuals with difficulty imaging indicate they don't easily see movement and are bewildered that some people see color in their imagery because they visualize in sepia tones! Beginning color imaging at the single letter level provides the brain with intensified imagery stimulation during a low level task.

Practice and Pacing

Practice the <u>Image</u> <u>Letters</u> step by either holding up a letter card or saying a sound. It is just as easily practiced in groups of children as in one-to-one treatment, with good group management. Group management to keep students actively involved may be as simple as 1) having all students writing in the air, and 2) requiring *thumbs up or down* responses from any students not called on to participate directly. Don't practice so long that the breath is taken out of the lesson, but do practice long enough to imprint the learning in the sensory system.

In pacing, the stimulus may only need to be for a few letters, but can be for many letters, depending on the needs of the student(s). Younger children, with less experience and exposure to letters, may need a considerable amount of stimulation, while older children or adults may need very little. The amount of stimulation is dependent on the sensory-cognitive needs of the student(s). Your pacing will be accurate if you understand the gestalt of why you are doing this, where it is going, and how much it is going to help with automaticity, self-correction, fluency, and confidence in reading and spelling.

In all pacing issues, be sure to overlap steps. Do some practice at this step, and if it seems sort of stable, overlap to the next step, while continuing this step—two steps working at the same time. Most important, don't belabor the stimulation. It is better to move too quickly than too slowly, because moving too slowly may take the joy and energy out of learning.

In teaching kindergarten children, the sheer joy and excitement they demonstrated regarding learning was astonishing as compared to sixth graders, where the innate joy and excitement seemed lost somewhere in the process of life and school. However, a teacher with positive energy, humor, and value for students can put joy and excitement back into learning. Pacing a sensory-cognitive program such as *Seeing Stars* requires the student to understand the process, be involved, and become active rather than passive in learning to learn. When more stimulation is needed at a given step, do it, but do it with an overlap into the next step—explaining where he or she is in the process of learning, *what* he or she is doing, and *why*.

Summary

Begin developing symbol imagery with the smallest unit of language—a letter—to establish a sensory-cognitive base of letter imagery from which to build into syllables. The imagery of a letter symbol should be taught with both the sound and letter name—and a label, if using the ADD Program.
The two steps of letter imagery are:

- *See*, image, say, and air-write
- *Hear*, image, say, and air-write

The *Seeing Stars* program may be integrated into any phonics or phonemic awareness programs. The concepts presented here will not confuse students using other phonics programs; developing this necessary sensory-cognitive base will enhance programs, not compete with them.

Summary:
Step 2
Imaging Letters

> **Goal:** Develop the ability to image, say, and write single letters by name and sound.

1. Imaging with a Letter Card
   - Teacher shows a card with a single letter, for approximately two seconds.
   - Student(s) says and writes the letter in the air, after the card is taken away.

2. Imaging without a Letter Card
   - Teacher says a sound.
   - Student(s) says and writes the letter in the air.

3. Keep in Mind
   - Saying and air-writing should be simultaneous.
   - Air-writing should be lower case.
   - Air-writing should be large enough to see a *shadow effect*.
   - If using the ADD Program, include the *labels* at any time.
   - Include with any phonics program.
   - Do some letter imagery in color.
   - Overlap to other *Seeing Stars* steps by continuing this step and starting the simple level of another.

Group Stimulation

Stimulating symbol imagery for a small group or whole classroom requires no modification of the steps; rather, it requires group management. Have the group or class respond as a whole, and then check various students to make sure they are processing. Call on specific individuals and have the other students give thumbs up or thumbs down for agreement or not, producing more attentive, active participants.

11

Imaging Syllable Cards

"I can't see anything. It's just dark up there," was the cry from Jan, a nineteen year old college student with weakness in both concept imagery and symbol imagery.

Jan was slowly conquering her weakness in phonemic awareness with articulatory feedback. Learning how to phonetically process words for reading and spelling, she was using her new skills, but it was slow. Not only did she have trouble decoding words, but she also had severe weakness in oral and written language comprehension. Though she always had a big smile on her face, she was failing in school and afraid for her future. It was another painful history. Elementary school through high school had been very difficult no matter how hard she tried, and her first year at a community college was resulting in frustration, embarrassment, and academic probation. Her goal of becoming a nurse was growing dim.

As the ADD and V/V Programs were initiated with Jan, she helped us understand an important first step in stimulating imagery. Unable to get past the darkness, we had to begin at a very basic level by having Jan actually *see* something and then image it. Soon she began to understand what it was to *visualize*. The Imaging Syllable Cards step provides the student with something to see and then image. The syllable stimulation begins with two sounds, either CV (consonant/vowel) or VC (vowel, consonant), and eventually moves to CCVCC.

73

The Structure of a Single Syllable

Seeing Stars applies imagery to sequencing sounds within *syllables*; thus, it is important to understand the structure of an English monosyllable. As defined in the ADD Program, there are two levels of a single syllable: *simple and complex*. A simple syllable does not have a blend, while a complex syllable has to have a blend; a blend being two consonant sounds together such as /st/, /sk/, /pl/, etc. In the example below, V = vowel, C = consonant, with words in parenthesis as examples of that syllable configuration. When you notice the sample words remember that /sh/ is one sound, as is /ay/, etc.

Simple Syllables	*Complex Syllables*
CV (to, by, she)	CCV (sky, play, blue)
VC (at, ash)	VCC (ask)
CVC (cat, ship)	CVCC (mask, lamp)
	CCVC (skip, black)
	CCVCC (stamp)

Though English syllables extend beyond the CCVCC level, as in the word *splits*, this program will primarily provide stimulation through the CCVCC level for imaging and sequencing sounds in a single syllable.

Nonword Syllable Cards

The Syllable Cards are nonword syllables to give students practice imaging and decoding, and extend from simple to complex patterns. Importantly, the syllable cards include irregular patterns that are often difficult for students to remember visually such as the vowel patterns of ai, ea, oa.

Pacing through the cards depends on the needs of your student(s), however, it is important to begin with the smallest units, such as VC or CV, and then move through the syllable structure as the student's syllable processing improves.

Here is Buzz beginning the Syllable Cards at the simple level, almost immediately after he demonstrated good ability to visualize isolated letters in the previous step.

SAMPLE LESSON

See and Image Syllables at the Simple Syllable Level

The Set

Nanci: *"I'm going to show you words to image, write in the air, and read to me. This is the second step in teaching you to visualize letters."*

Buzz: "OK." (Small voice.)

Lesson

Nanci: *"Here we go."* (*I hold up the card* **ap**, *one second for each letter, then take it away.*)

Nanci: *"What letters did you see?*

Buzz: "**A-P**."

Nanci: *"Great. Now every time we do that I want you to say and write the letters in the air. Like this."* (I demonstrate saying and writing the letters.)

Buzz: "OK. **A-P**." (Saying and writing the letters.)

Nanci: *"What would that word say?"*

Buzz: *"Ap."*

Nanci: *"See, your brain can do this. Now what was the last letter you saw?"*

Buzz: "The **P**."

Nanci: *"Right! What was the first one you saw!?"*

Buzz: Eyes looking up. "This is easy. The **A**."

Nanci: *"Yes! Yes!"*

Having the student read the pattern will help improve his word attack skills but, more importantly Buzz has to hold the word a little longer in his imagination, preparation for the *hold and compare* function needed for self-correction.

Nanci: *"Here's another one."* (I hold up the nonword card **ib**.)

Buzz: "**I-B**...*ib*." (Saying and writing at the same time.)

Having the student decode the pattern from imagery will help improve word attack skills and hold the word a little longer in his imagination — preparation for the *hold and compare* function needed for self-correction.

Lesson Summary:
See and Image Syllables at the Simple Syllable Level

- Teacher shows syllable card , one second for each letter.
- Student(s) sees, says letter names, and writes in the air.
- Student(s) reads the nonword syllable from memory.
- Teacher asks student(s) to recall a specific letter by its number in the syllable.
- Saying letter names and writing should be done simultaneously.
- Student(s) air-writes in *lower case letters.*
- Student(s) air-writes *large enough* to see a "shadow" effect.

Though Buzz did well in the lesson above, an interactive program where questions are asked and responses given will ultimately produce student errors. Error handling requires responding to the response and always has the same frame: note the response, come in on a positive, and start your questioning *where the student is* (not where you want them to be). Here are some examples of error handling.

Error:
Buzz says back the wrong letters.

SAMPLE LESSON

Error Handling at the Simple Syllable Level

I hold up the card **ak**. Buzz says back the wrong letters.

Nanci: *"Here's another one."*

Nanci: *"What letters did you see?*

Buzz: **"A-P."**

Nanci: *"If you saw an **A** and a **P**, that would look like this…I write out **a-p**. Let's look at the card again and see if that matches."*

Buzz: "Oh, it is **A–K**." (Looking again at the card and comparing it with his response.)

Nanci: *"Right! Here is what **A-P** looks like and here is what **A-K** looks like. Let's do another one."*

By handling the error in this manner of responding to the response, Buzz is able to compare his response with the stimulus. He feels valued because I am acknowledging his thinking every time he responds, in contrast to, "No, that's not **A-P**, that's **A-K**!" Also, I am modeling the hold and compare process he will need to use to self-correct in contextual reading and elsewhere.

I hold up the card **fip**. Buzz says back wrong letters again, and I direct to a specific letter.

Nanci: *"Here's another one."*

Nanci: *"What letters did you see?*

Buzz: **F-E-P**."

Nanci: *"If it was **F-E-P** it would look like this. (I write out fep.)*

"Let's look at the card again and see if that matches every letter, especially think about the middle letter."

*(I show the **fip** card again.)*

Buzz: Looking again at the card and comparing it with his response, he says, "Oh, it is **F-I-P**."

I hold up the card **fip**. Buzz reads the word from memory—wrong.

Nanci: *"What letters did you see?"*

Buzz: **F-I-P**."

Nanci: *"Right! And, what would that say?"*

Error:
Buzz says back wrong letters again, and I direct to a specific letter.

Error:
Buzz reads the word from memory—wrong.

Buzz: "*Fap.*"

Nanci: *"When you say fap, what vowel do you hear and visualize in the middle?"*

Buzz: "f...a...p. /a/. And the letter **A** says /a/, so the word you showed me would be *fip.*"

Hmmm, pretty easy to correct, but his response might need more work such as:

I hold up the card **fip**.

Nanci: *"What letters did you see?*

Buzz: "**F–I–P**."

Nanci: *"Right! And, what would that say?"*

Buzz: "*Fap.*"

Nanci: *"When you say fap, what vowel do you hear and visualize in the middle?"*

Buzz: "f...a...p. /i/."

He is probably visually remembering the letter **I**, rather than perceiving the sound. So you would need to respond to his response like this, beginning with a positive.

Nanci: *"There was the letter **I** in the word. What sound does it make?*

Buzz: "/i/."

Nanci: *"Right. (I hold up the **fip** card for him to read as he looks at it, rather than from memory.) So if the **I** says /i/, what will the word say?"*

Buzz: "*Fip.*"

Nanci: *"Right. That's perfect. Let's learn from what you first said, for instance, when you said fap awhile ago, what letter had to be in the middle?"*

Buzz: "The letter **A**, because it says /a/."

Nanci: *"Right and the word would look like this."* (I write out fap.)

Hmmm…still seems somewhat easy…here Buzz can't perceive sounds in syllables, thus he can't tell if he has said the right sound or not:

*I hold up the card **fip**.*

Nanci: *"What letters did you see?*

Buzz: **"F-I-P**."

Nanci: *"Right! And, what would that say?"*

Buzz: *"Fap."*

Nanci: *"When you say fap, what sound do you hear in the middle and what letter do you see for it? Say each sound, and touch one of your fingers for each sound."*

(If you are using the ADD Program, the *labels* would enable the student to have a concrete experience of feeling the sounds, thus your language would be, 'What do you *feel* after the lip cooler.')

Buzz: "f…a…p." (Buzz isolates each sound on three fingers of his hand.) "Oh, the middle sound is /a/."

Nanci: *"Right. And what letter says /a/?"*

Buzz: **"A**. It would have to be an **A** in there."

Nanci: *"Right. Look at the word card again. (I show the card **fip**).*

"Touch and say the vowel sound first, then touch and say it with the letter after it."

Buzz: (Looking at the card **fip**, touching each letter.) "/i/…/ip/."

Nanci: *"Great, now say and touch all three sounds."*

80

	Buzz:	(Looking at the card **fip**, touching each letter.) "f…i…p."
	Nanci:	*"Great. Look at the card again and say them altogether."*
Responding to the response stimulates *holding and comparing*.	Buzz:	*"Fip."*
	Nanci:	*"Now, let's finish with that imaging part again. Say fip and tell me what letter you picture for the vowel!"*
	Buzz:	*"Fip. An **I**!"*
	Nanci:	*"Right! Right! Right! You're getting this! You're brain's going to visualize letters easily."*

No matter where he goes, you can respond to his response; and his learning will be increased by the holding and comparing he is doing in matching his response to the stimulus.

Practice and Pacing: Overlap between Steps!

It is important to overlap steps when pacing *Seeing Stars*. As Buzz improves his ability to see and image from the VC level of cards, he should be moved to the CV and CVC level of a simple syllable. This may take a few sessions or a few moments—all depending on his response to the stimulation. As he is moved into the complex level of the syllable cards, he'll be overlapped at the simple syllable level to the Imaging and Sequencing Syllables step (See Chapter 12). Thus, he is doing two steps at the same time: 1) seeing the card and imaging and 2) imaging and sequencing sounds in syllables. The tasks given at the Syllable Cards level can be more difficult than the tasks at the Imaging and Sequencing Syllables; retrieving an image is easier than creating one.

Imaging supports phonemic awareness as was discussed in the concept section of this book. To develop phonemic sequencing for blends, *seeing* letters of blends on a card, *holding* them in imagery, and *retrieving* them by visualizing, verbalizing, and writing in the air aids in the integration of the imagery and phonemic awareness systems.

The following is a sample lesson at the complex level to demonstrate the simplicity of extending the student into complex patterns, including irregular spelling patterns for vowels. Remember, you would not extend a student into CCVCC patterns unless you had initiated the <u>Imaging</u> and <u>Sequencing</u> <u>Syllables</u> step of *Seeing Stars*. *Keep the syllable cards just a little ahead of the sequencing sounds step.*

| ┌─────────────────────────────┐ |
| **SAMPLE LESSON** |

See and Image Syllables at the Complex Syllable Level

The Set

Begin teaching spelling patterns from the syllable cards.

Nanci: *"Here are some more words, only now we're teaching your brain to visualize more and more letters, and also patterns of letters to help you with spelling."*

Buzz: "OK."

Lesson

Nanci: *"Here we go. Say and write the letters, please!"* (*I hold up the card **pli**, one second for each letter, then take it away.*)

Buzz: "**p-l-i**." (Saying and writing the letters, *not the sounds*, at the same time.)

Nanci: *"What would that word say?"*

Buzz: *"Pli."*

Nanci: *"Great. What was the second letter you saw?"*

Buzz: "Hmmm. An **L**.

Nanci: *"Excellent. Here's another one."* (*I hold up the card **eask**.*)

Buzz: "**e-a-s-k**." (Saying and writing the letters.)

Nanci: *"What would that word say?"*

Buzz: *"eask."*

Check imagery for specific letters: "What was the second letter you saw?"

Nanci: *"Right. That's the two vowels go walking rule you have heard about before. It goes like this: When two vowels go walking the first on does the talking, so the letter **E** had to say its name."*

Buzz: "I've heard that rule for years."

Nanci: *"Right. Now we'll practice it with imagery. What was the second letter you saw?"*

Buzz: "What was the word, again."

Nanci: *"You probably do need to see it again because we talked in between." (I hold up the **eask** card again, and take it away.)*

Buzz: "The second letter was **A**."

Doing a few more, Buzz seems good at this level of CCV and VCC with a blend on either side of the vowel. I decide to extend him into CCVC and CVCC.

Have the student decode the word from imagery: "What would that word say?"

Nanci: *"We've done a number of those with three sounds, now let's try four!" (I hold up the card **flep**.)*

Buzz: "**f-l-e-p**." (Saying and writing the letters.)

Nanci: *"What would that word say?"*

Buzz: "*flep*."

Nanci: *"GREAT! Here's another one." (I hold up the card **spup**.)*

Buzz: "**s-p-u-p**." (Saying and writing the letters.)

Nanci: *"What would that word say?"*

Buzz: "*spup*."

Nanci: *"GREAT! Here's another one." (I hold up the card **smait**.)*

Buzz: "**s-m-a-i-t**." (Saying and writing the letters.)

Nanci: *"What would that word say?"*

Buzz: "*smait*."

Nanci: *"What's the fourth letter you see?"*

Buzz: "**I**." (Small hand up, counting the letters he is imaging.)

We do a few more at the CCVC level and then try some CVCC.

Nanci: *"GREAT! Here's another one."* (I hold up the card **masp**.)

Buzz: "**m-a-s-p**." (Saying and writing the letters.)

Nanci: *"What would that word say?"*

Buzz: *"masp."*

Nanci: *"Good job, you're getting these with four letters, let's try some more!* (I hold up the card **creats**.)

Buzz: "**C-R-E-A-T-S**" (Saying and writing the letters.)

Nanci: *"What would that word say?"*

Buzz: *"Creats."*

Nanci: *"Great. Remember we're just doing this to help you read and spell better and you've improved from three letters to five, pretty soon we'll be up to six and seven letters!*

Buzz: "Hmmm."

Lesson Summary:
See and Image Syllables at the Complex Syllable Level

- Teacher shows syllable card , one second for each letter.
- Student(s) sees, says letter names, and writes in the air.
- Student(s) reads the nonword from memory.
- Teacher asks student(s) to recall a specific letter by its number in the syllable.
- Begin overlap into slightly irregular spelling patterns.

Buzz practiced imaging and air-writing from the cards for a short period of time, approximately ten minutes, or the equivalent of about ten to twenty cards. Though he did very well in the above lesson, the following is a demonstration lesson to improve your error handling technique. The type of error is identified at the beginning of each example.

```
╔══════════════════════════════════════╗
║            SAMPLE  LESSON             ║
╚══════════════════════════════════════╝
```

Error Handling at the Complex Level

Error:
Buzz says wrong the letter.

I hold up the card spoif. Buzz says wrong the letter.

Nanci: *"Here's another one."*

Nanci: *"What letters did you see?*

Buzz: **"S-P-O-I-T."**

Nanci: *"If it was **S-P-O-I-T** it would look like this."* (I write out spoit.) *"Let's look at the card again and see if that matches every letter."* (I show the **spoif** card again.)

Buzz: "Oh, it is **S-P-O-I-F**." (Looking at the card again and comparing it with his response.)

Nanci: *"Right! And, what would that say?"*

Buzz: *"Spoif."*

Error:
Buzz decodes the word wrong.

I hold up the card spoif. Buzz decodes the word wrong.

Nanci: *"Here's another one."*
Nanci: *"What letters did you see?*

Buzz: **"S-P-O-I-F."**

Nanci: *"Right! And, what would that say?"*

Buzz: *"Spoil."*

Nanci: *"If is said spoil, what letter would you see last?"*

Buzz: *"Spoil...oh, an **L**. Can I see the card again?"*

Nanci: *"Sure."* (*I show him the card* **spoif***, one second for each letter, and then take it away.*)

Buzz: "Oh, I see an **F** at the end. *Spoif!*"

Nanci: *"Right, you needed to hear the /f/ on the end."*

Incorporating into the ADD Program

This level of stimulation lends itself easily to the articulatory feedback and labels of the ADD Program as assistance with sensory feedback and error handling. Just as symbol imagery helps concretize phonemes, the ADD Program develops articulatory feedback to give a concrete experience to phonemes. When the articulatory feedback is labeled, such as "lip popper," "tip tapper," the language describes the sensory experience, and the language/labels can be used to assist in error handling feedback. For example, ask for a label along with a letter name, to bring in articulatory feedback.

SAMPLE LESSON

Decoding Error, Incorporating ADD Program labels

Nanci: *"Here's another one."* (*I hold up the card spoif.*) *"What letters did you see?*

Buzz: "S-P-O-I-F."

Nanci: *"Right! And, what would that say?"*

Buzz: "Spoit."

Nanci: *"If it said spoit, label what you feel last."*

Buzz: "Spoit, a tip tapper."

Nanci: *"Right. And what letter would you need to see last?"*

Buzz: "T. Can I see the card again?"

Nanci: *"Sure."* (*I show him the card spoif and then take it away.*)

Buzz: "Spoif!"

Nanci: *"Right!, you needed to feel the lip cooler on the end."*

86

Referring Buzz to his mouth by using the ADD program labels gives him a concrete experience from which to match his response to the stimulus. As symbol imagery is developed, he will need to rely less on the articulatory experience and be able to quickly judge the match by *visual patterns*. For example, if I'm reading *spoif* and mistakenly say "spoit" my symbol imagery is so strong that I visualize the letter **T** on the end, and I don't have to check my mouth for verification. However, if my processing is severely impaired, or *while* my symbol imagery is still developing, a program such as the ADD program consciously calls articulatory feedback to my attention. Using it enables me to have a concrete sensory experience from which to match until my symbol imagery can take over and more rapidly give me feedback. It is infinitely more time consuming to check my mouth for verification than to check my imagery, which, once developed just pops in my head instantly; but until I have that imagery, my mouth is my key to verification.

Summary

The Syllable Cards step begins developing syllable symbol imagery with visual stimulation—students *see* a syllable, ranging from simple to complex, and say and write what they imaged. Rather than creating the imagery from an auditory stimulus, this step allows the sensory system to retrieve an image. Once images are visualized and verbalized, students decode the syllable from memory—strengthening both decoding and visual memory for letters.

The error handling technique of responding to the response enhances sensory input. As the students are imaging letters on the syllable cards at the simple syllable level, they are overlapped to the next step at the simple level. Thus, two *Seeing Stars* steps are combined, the Syllable Card step always slightly ahead of the sound sequencing step—the next chapter.

Summary: Step 3

Imaging Syllable Cards

Goal: Develop the ability to image, write, and decode simple and complex nonsense words, including irregular spelling patterns.

---

1. Syllable Words are nonword single syllable words ranging from CV to CCVCC syllables, including irregularities such as ai, ea, oa, tch, ck, etc.

2. The structure of an English single syllable can be simple or complex:

Simple Syllables	*Complex Syllables*
CV	CCV
VC	VCC
CVC	CVCC
	CCVC
	CCVCC

3. Begin with simple syllable cards.

4. Lesson Summary:
   - Teacher shows syllable card , one second for each letter.
   - Student(s) sees, says letter names, and writes in the air.
   - Student(s) reads the nonword syllable from memory.
   - Saying letter names and writing should be done simultaneously.
   - Student(s) air-writes in lower case letters.
   - Student(s) air-writes *large enough* to see a "shadow" effect.

5. Error handle by responding to the response to give more opportunity to develop independent and rapid sensory-cognitive processing.

6. Pace by overlapping to the next Seeing Stars step, <u>Imaging</u> <u>and</u> <u>Sequencing</u> <u>Syllables</u> at a slightly lower level.

Group Stimulation

The <u>Imaging Syllable Cards</u> step can easily be used with a small group or whole classroom and *requires no modification of the process,* only group management techniques. Have the group or class respond as a whole, and then check various students to be sure they are imaging and air-writing appropriately. Call on specific individuals and have the other students give thumbs up or thumbs down to ensure active attention.

Imaging & Sequencing Syllables:
Syllable Board

The goal of the <u>Imaging and Sequencing Syllables</u> step is to develop the *hold and compare process necessary for self-correcting and fluency in reading and spelling.* Hold and compare means just what it seems: to hold one pattern and compare it with another—to hold the old pattern and compare it with the new—to hold your response and compare it with the stimulus. The ability to hold and compare is critical to self-correction and self-correction is critical to independence in reading and spelling. Without self-correction we are dependent on someone else to judge whether we are right or wrong. Without the ability to self-correct, we have lost control of our cognitive independence, a most precious gift.

When I look at the word *stream* (the stimulus) do I match when I say *"steam"* (the response)? What parts of my sensory system allow me to *know* that I have matched or mismatched? One answer is my phonemic awareness. Being able to judge sounds within syllables allows me to process my response as compared to the stimulus. A second answer is my symbol imagery. Being able to rapidly image letters allows me to rapidly judge sounds through imagery and thus match response to stimulus more quickly. I can rapidly image the letters in my response of "steam" and instantaneously *see* that the **r** wasn't there and thus didn't match the stimulus.

The issue of timing, of rapidly being able to judge response to stimulus, is a critical factor in self-correction and cognitive independence. If the processing of stimulus to response is slow, we often yield to a guessing strategy or to inattention.

This <u>Imaging and Sequencing Syllables</u> part of *Seeing Stars* has three steps, moving from simple through complex patterns:

1) Imaging and writing on the *syllable board*
2) Imaging and air-writing *with* a chain

3) Imaging and air-writing *without* a chain

The Syllable Board shows *sounds as units represented by letters*. The board has seven designated units on which the student writes imaginary letters. The words are given to the student in a chain, with one sound changing at a time. Giving the student a chain simplifies the task while focusing on the development of the hold and compare process.

Using the syllable board is simple. The teacher says a syllable and the student says and writes the word on the syllable board with his or her finger, creating imaginary letters on each unit. The next syllable is presented to the student, with only one sound changed, again the student writes the new imaginary pattern on the board. Writing imaginary letters is much less threatening than writing those that can be seen and judged for either accuracy or penmanship, or both!

The following lesson demonstrates Buzz *Visualizing and Verbalizing* (dual coding) and representing a syllable with imaginary letters. I begin the lesson with a VC chain, hoping that little time will be needed here since he was very successful at VC with the syllable cards.

SAMPLE LESSON

Syllable Board at the VC Level

The Set

Nanci: *"Here we go with a new task. You get to write imaginary letters on this board! Remember to say and write just as you did when I showed you a card. OK?"*

Buzz: "OK. You say a word and I write it, but with no pencil!!??"

"Just use the tip of your finger to write the word, and always try to visualize as you write."

Nanci: *"No pencil. Just use the tip of your finger to write the word, and always try to visualize as you write. Remember, we're developing that imagery part of your brain to help you with reading and spelling."*

Lesson

Buzz: "Right. I'm ready!"

Nanci: *"Ip. Say the word back to me, write it on the syllable board, and say the letters as you write!"*

Buzz: "*Ip*…**I-P**." (He writes the word with the tip of his finger on the syllable board, and says each letter name as he writes.)

"...what was the last letter you saw?"

Nanci: *"Great. Now for the fun part, what was the last letter you saw?"*

Buzz: "**P**! This is just like when we did the cards!"

Nanci: *"Right. And here's another thing like on the cards. Read the word from memory."*

"Only one sound will change at a time."

Buzz: "*Ip.*"

Nanci: *"Great. Your memory and decoding are both getting better! Let's do some more. Only one sound will change at a time. Change ip to iv."*

Buzz: "*Iv*…**I-V**. (He says and write the letters on the board.) Do you want me to tell you what it says?"

"Can you still see it in your imagination and read it to me?"

Nanci: *"Yes! Can you still see it in your imagination and read it to me?"*

Buzz: "*Iv*. I can remember it. And, read it."

Nanci: *"Great again! Here's another one. Change iv to ig."*

Buzz: "*Ig*…**I-G**." (He says and write the letters on the board.)

Nanci: *"Good job. See, this isn't difficult and the imagery part of your brain is getting lots of exercise—and, when you go to spell words it'll be easier for you to remember what they look like!*

"Before I give you a few more, what was the first letter you saw?"

Buzz: "Hmmm. An **I**." (He momentarily looked up to retrieve his imagery.)

Nanci: *"Yup. Change ig to og."*

Buzz: "The **I** changes to an **O**. *Og*...**O-G**." (He says and writes on the syllable board.)

Nanci: *"Right. And what does that say?*

Buzz: "*Og*."

Nanci: *"Really good. Change og to om."*

Buzz: "*Om*...the **G** changes to an **M**. **O-M**."

Nanci: *"What's the last letter you have now?"*

Buzz: "**M**."

Nanci: *"Good job!"*

Lesson Summary:
Syllable Board at the VC Level

- Teacher says a syllable.

- Student(s) repeats the nonword syllable.

- Student(s) says and writes imaginary letters on the syllable board.

- Student(s) reads the nonword from memory.

- Teacher asks student(s) to recall a specific letter by its number in the syllable.

- Remember:

  Saying letter names and writing should be done simultaneously.

  Student(s) writes in *lower case letters.*

  Student(s) writes *large enough* to see a "shadow" effect.

Since interaction creates responses, and responses create the possibility of error, here are a few sample error handling lessons. Buzz doesn't always make a response that I can respond to, so some of these sample error handling examples also illustrate picking up on a positive and then demonstrating the appropriate response.

SAMPLE LESSON

Error Handling for Simple Level of Syllable Board

Error:
Buzz doesn't remember the word.

Error: Buzz doesn't say letters as he writes:

Nanci: *"Ip. Say the word back to me, write it on the syllable board, and say the letters as you write!"*

Buzz: *"Ip."* (He writes the word with the tip of his finger on the syllable board.)

Nanci: *"You did a good job of saying the word and writing the letters, next time say the letters as you write*

---

	the word. Like this. (I demonstrate for him how to say the word ip before beginning to write, and then when writing I say each letter as I write.)
	Buzz: "Oh, yeah. Just like when we did the cards. *Ip*…**I-P**. (He writes the word again and says each letter name.)
	Nanci: *"Great. Now for the fun part, what was the last letter you saw?"*
Error: **Buzz doesn't say letters as he writes.**	*Error: Buzz doesn't remember the word.*
	Nanci: *"Change ip to iv."*
	Buzz: "What was the word again? I forgot what you said!"
	Nanci: *"That's OK, as you get better at imaging, remembering will get easier. But, for now, here's something that will help you.*
"… as imaging gets easier, remembering will get easier."	*"Say the old word and then the new word, like this: ip to iv and write the letters as you say it. Focus on seeing that imaginary last letter."*
	Buzz: *"Ip to iv*…Oh, I got it…**I-V**." (He says and write the letters.)
	Nanci: *"Good job. Like I said, as imaging gets easier, remembering will get easier. "*

The following lesson extends the syllable board stimulation into CVC. Naturally, pacing depends on the student's response, with younger students or those with more severe weakness *perhaps* moving more slowly will be necessary. Perhaps not.

This lesson further demonstrates how to apply the two common reading and spelling rules to symbol imagery stimulation: the final e and the two vowels go walking rule. The "final e" rule is: when the letter **e** comes at the end of a word, it can jump over a letter (or sound) and make the vowel say its name—*at* becomes *ate*, *Sam* becomes *same*, *Tim* becomes *time*, etc. The letter **e** has a function at the end of words, it is not just silent. "When two vowels go walking, the first one does the talking" rule is just what it says: when two vowels are together, the first one says its name—**ai** says **A** like in aim, **oa** says **O** like in oat, **ea** says **E** like in eat. The two vowels go walking rule is fairly consistent in English and naturally doesn't apply to vowel combinations that have their own sounds such as oi, oy, ou, ow, au, aw. The letters should be written in a separate space for each letter, even though two letters make one sound. These two rules could have been applied at the VC level, just as easily as here. It is your choice; however, I generally don't start rules until the student has experienced success in lessons with regular spelling patterns.

SAMPLE LESSON

Syllable Board at the CV and CVC Level

The Set

Nanci: *"You're doing really well with two sounds, let's keep going and see if we can get to three sounds."*

Buzz: "I bet I can."

Lesson

Nanci: *"Fi. Say the word back to me and write it on the syllable board. Remember to say the letters as you write."*

Buzz: *"Fi...***F-I***."* (He writes the word with the tip of his finger on the syllable board, and says each letter name as he writes.)

Nanci: *"Great. What was the last letter you saw and what does the word say?"*

Buzz: "**I**...*fi.*"

Nanci: *"Right. Change fi to ki."*

Buzz: *"Ki...***K-I***."* (He says and write the letters on the syllable board.)

Nanci: *"Can you still see it in your imagination and read it to me?"*

"What was the last letter you saw and what does the word say?"

Buzz: "*Ki.*"

Nanci: *"Great. Here's another one. Change ki to kif."*

Buzz: "*Kif...***K-I-F**." (He says and write the letters on the syllable board.)

Nanci: *"Good job. What was the second letter you saw?"*

Buzz: "Hmmm. An **I**."

Nanci: *"Yes, indeed. Change kif to koof."*

Buzz: "The **I** changes to **OO**. **K-O-O-F**." (He says and writes on the syllable board, using two spaces for the two **O**'s.)

Nanci: *"Right. And what does that say?"*

Buzz: "*Koof.*"

Nanci: *"Really good. Change Koof to foof."*

Buzz: "*Foof...*the **K** changes to an **F**. **F-O-O-F**."

Nanci: *"What's the third letter you see?"*

Buzz: "**O**."

Nanci: *"Great. Here's another one. Change foof to faef."*

Buzz: "*Faef...***F-A-F-E**." (He says and write the letters on the syllable board.)

Nanci: *"Good job. What was the last letter you saw?"*

Buzz: "An **E**."

Nanci: *"What other letters could we use to make the letter **A** say its name?"*

Buzz: "We could use an **E** after the **A**.

Nanci: *"Yes, we could but it's not very common. In other words, we won't see it written that way very often when we read or spell. What is that other way you've seen on our cards that makes the **A** says its name?"*

"What other letters could we use to make the letter A say its name?"

"What is that other way you've seen on our cards that makes the A says its name?"

Buzz: "Oh, the **ai**!" (If he couldn't retrieve it, I would show him a card with **ai** on it to refresh his visual memory.)

Nanci: *"Yes! Write faef with those letters in the middle."*

Buzz: "**F-A-I-F**."

Nanci: *"Yes, indeed. Change faef to faf."*

Buzz: "The **I** goes away. **F-A-F**." (He says and writes on the syllable board.)

Nanci: *"Right. And what does that say?*

Buzz: *"Faf."*

Nanci: *"Really good. Change faf to fat."*

Buzz: "*Fat*…the last **F** changes to a **T**. **F-A-T**. A real word!"

Nanci: *"Right! What's the second letter you see?"*

Buzz: "**A**."

Nanci: *"Good job!"*

Lesson Summary:
Syllable Board at the CV and CVC Level

- Teacher says a syllable.

- Student(s) repeats the nonword syllable.

- Student(s) says and writes imaginary letters on the syllable board.

- Student(s) reads the nonword from memory.

- Teacher asks student(s) to recall a specific letter by its number in the syllable.

- Use "Final e" and "Two vowels go walking rule," each letter written on a separate unit space.

Practice and Pacing

Simple and complex syllables are practiced on the syllable board; and practice should be continued until students demonstrate a level of automaticity, but not until they are crazed with boredom! *The secret to good pacing is overlapping steps.*

Mastery is accuracy with automaticity; meaning, students complete the task correctly as quickly and easily as you can. Their sensory system can process information automatically. Automaticity can be thought of as "timing" factor. As stated earlier, if students need too much time to do a task, it means they are having to *think* their way through the task; thus, they are not automatic in their processing. This applies to all areas of sensory-cognitive processing, including concept imagery and symbol imagery. The imagery side of dual coding needs to happen automatically—rapid imaging of the concepts or the detail so that imagery is quickly integrated with language. It is difficult to interpret, comprehend, and reason, if the basic processing of imagery is not quick and automatic. Practice until a step is automatic but overlap steps to keep energy in the stimulation.

With that in mind, as students are *becoming* able to write a simple syllable on the sequencing board, overlap to *imaging and air-writing with a chain* at the simple level. It is important to notice that the overlap here is at the same level. The stimulus task changes, not the level. When students can process a simple syllable, then both the Syllable Board and the *image and write* tasks are extended to the complex syllable.

Summary

Stimulating Imagery and Sequencing in Syllables begins with the Syllable Board, designating the units for letters. As students are presented a chain of syllables, from simple through complex, they write imaginary letters on the board, one letter for each line on the board. If you don't have a *Seeing Stars* Syllable Board, one can easily be made from card stock by designating the left of the board and lines for the letter units.

Proper error handling is directly related to progress, and is demonstrated in this chapter and the previous chapter. The issue of starting with a positive, and responding to the response, is the same for all symbol imagery stimulation, and all Lindamood-Bell programs. It takes practice, but learning how to do it can benefit many areas of instruction and interaction.

Practice and pacing are determined by the needs of the student(s), but in general the best pacing is achieved by overlapping steps. In the Syllable Board stimulation this is very important. The Syllable Board step should be overlapped to the next step of <u>Imaging</u> and <u>Air-Writing with a Chain</u>.

Summary: Step 4

Imaging & Sequencing Syllables: Syllable Board

> **Goal:** To develop symbol imagery for sequencing sounds in words, and beginning exposure to irregularities.

1. Student writes imaginary letters on the syllable board, starting from left to right.

2. The syllable board has designated units, place holders, for imaged letters.

3. Each letter has a separate space on the board, including digraphs, diphthongs, etc.

4. The stimulation moves from simple to complex syllables.

5. A chain of syllables is presented (one sound changing at time) to develop the hold and compare process.

6. Writing imaginary letters is less threatening than writing on paper!

7. Use common irregularities, such as the "final e" and "two vowels go walking" rule.

8. Pace by overlapping to the next step of Image and Air-Write at the same syllable level.

Lesson Summary:
Syllable Board

- Teacher says a syllable.

- Student(s) repeats the nonword syllable.

- Student(s) says and writes imaginary letters on the syllable board.

- Student(s) reads the nonword from memory.

- Teacher asks student(s) to recall a specific letter by its number in the syllable.

- Use "final e" and "two vowels go walking" rule.

- Remember:

    Saying letter names and writing should be done simultaneously.

    Student(s) writes in lower case letters.

    Student(s) writes large enough to see a "shadow" effect.

Group Instruction

Small or large group instruction does not require changing the steps for the syllable board stimulation. Each student has a board to use, whether in small groups or the entire class. Students choose the Syllable Board at the beginning of the lesson, or may have their own in their desk. As the teacher says the syllables, students are called on randomly for answers and other students give thumbs up or down to demonstrate their feedback to the response. Small groups of students often verbalize in unison, a small choir—fun if classroom teacher has previously established good control and rapport.

Imaging & Sequencing Syllables: Air-Write *with* a Chain

The Air-Write with a Chain step extends into a slightly more difficult task of writing in the air without the aid of a board visually designating units. When using the syllable board, Buzz had a space in which to write the letter, while this helped him see letters as units, he now needs to image and write without the concreteness of the board. This is the real world for Buzz's sensory system—neither a board nor colored blocks designating the units. The syllable board is a means to an end, a method to stimulate the sensory system and develop the ability to self-correct, but not an end in itself.

There are two parts of the Air-Writing with a Chain stimulation: 1) the student hears the whole word and writes in the air (imaging the parts from the whole), and 2) the student hears each letter and writes in the air (imaging the whole from the parts). The latter seems to be more difficult.

First, the student is given a chain of nonwords to image and write in the air. Simultaneous saying and writing continues, as well as writing in medium size lower case letters. Note whether the student is actually forming the letters he or she is saying, but do not correct the manner in which the letter is formed such as from down to up, etc. In symbol imagery development it is important the student write from left to right, in lower case, medium sized letters; but, it is not important that a letter be formed according to a certain motor planning sequence.

There are four symbol imagery exercises at the image and air-write step:

1) *Decode the Syllable*
   The student reads his or her imaged pattern. Teacher dialogue: "Say what you see" or "Read the word."

2) *Identify a Specific Letter*

The student identifies a requested letter in the imaged word. Teacher dialogue: "What is the third letter you see?"

3) *Say Letters Backwards*
Student says the letters backwards from the imaged word. Teacher dialogue: "Tell me the letters you see backwards." (Student does not write backwards, just says backwards.)

4) *Manipulate Letters*
Student manipulates the letters as requested by the teacher. Teacher dialogue: "Take out the **T** and put in a **K**. Now, say what you see?"

The following is a sample lesson (whole to parts) using the symbol imagery exercises, and calling attention to some spelling irregularities.

Whole to Parts:
Teacher says word
student images each letter.

SAMPLE LESSON

Imaging and Air-Writing with a Chain at the Simple CVC Level (Whole to Parts)

The Set

Nanci: *"Now, we're going to do the same thing, but without the board. We can use the board again later, if we want. But, now just write them in the air!"*

Buzz: *"OK."*

Lesson

Nanci: *"What letters do you see when I say the word, teb. Say the word back to me, write it in the air...and, as usual, say the letters as you write."*

Buzz: *"Teb...**T-E-B**."* (He writes the word in the air and says each letter name as he writes.)

Identifying a letter by order in the syllable:

Nanci: *"Great. See, this is just the same as using the syllable board, only now it is in the air. What was the last letter you saw?"*

Buzz: "**B**. Yes, this is just the same. Easy!"

Nanci: *"Right. And here's another thing like on the cards and the board. Read the word from memory!"*

Buzz: "Easy. *Teb.* I can still see it in my imagination!"

Nanci: *"Oh, you're just a champ! Let's do some more. We'll do all kinds of fun things, like using the final e rule, the two vowels rule, all those things. Change teb to tesh."*

Buzz: "*Tesh*…**T-E-S-H**. (He says and write the letters in the air.) Do you want me to tell you what it says?"

Nanci: *"Yes! Can you?"*

Buzz: "*Tesh!*"

Nanci: *"Great again! What's the third letter you see?"*

Buzz: "An **S**."

Saying the letters backwards:

Nanci: *"Right. You're getting good at this, tell me the letters you see, but instead of saying them from start to finish, go from finish to start—go backwards."*

Buzz: "Hmmm. Like this? **H-S-E-T**. (Saying each letter, but *not* writing in the air.)

Nanci: *"Yes. Doing that little task forces you to really visualize the word and hold it long enough to say the letters! It is good exercise for your word imagination!"*

Buzz: "OK."

Nanci: *"OK. And, what was the second letter you saw—going front to back, of course."*

Student says letters backwards:

"…tell me the letters you see… backwards."

Buzz: "Easy. It was the **E**. **T-E-S-H**. And, it says tesh."

Nanci: *"Right. Here's another one. Change tesh to teesh."*

Buzz: *"Teesh*...Add an **A** after the **E**—ea! **T-E-A-S-H**." (He says and write the letters in the air.)

Nanci: *"Good job. If you had said* **T-E-E-S-H**, *that would have been correct also. Unfortunately, in English we have to learn to spell words more than one way in order to be right. So, let's leave this word with* **ea** *in the middle, and go on.*

"Like, say the letters in *teesh* again to me so I know you have it."

Buzz: **"T-E-A-S-H**."

Student says each letter backwards, but does not write backwards!

Nanci: *"Great. Now say them backwards!"*

Buzz: **"H-S-A-E-T**." (He *says* each letter, but does not write backwards...I am not teaching him to write from right to left!)

Nanci: *"Good. Good. Good. Now, what is the third letter you see?"*

Buzz: **"A**."

Nanci: *"And, what does it say?"*

Buzz: *"Teash*!"

"Take out the S and put in a C, and what does it say?"

Teacher manipulates and student reads:

Nanci: *"Great. Take out the* **S** *and put in a* **C**, *and what does it say?"*

Buzz: "Hmmm (eyes up, visualizing). *Teach*!"

Nanci: *"Yes! Now, write that in the air...please!"*

Buzz: **"T-E-A-C-H**." (Saying and writing in the air.)

Nanci: *"Excellent. Let's do a few more. Change teach to teaf."*

Buzz: "The **CH** changes to an **F**. **T-E-A-F**." (He says and writes.)

Nanci: *"Right. And what does that say?*

Buzz: *"Teaf."*

Nanci: *"Really good. Backwards, please.*

Buzz: "**F-A-E-T**."

Nanci: *"Second letter you see."* (Remember, he never saw the letters in reverse or wrote them in reverse! It only looks weird here in print!)

Buzz: "Hmmm. An **E**."

Nanci: *"And, what's the word say?"*

Buzz: *"Teaf.* Like the real word, leaf. All I'd have to do is change the **T** to an **L**!

Nanci: *"Right. You're doing so well. Let's start putting what is called blends in our words, where two consonant sounds come together. Maybe we'll use the syllable board to start that and then go to writing in the air…or maybe not."*

Lesson Summary:
Imaging and Air Writing with a Chain at the Simple CVC Level

- Teacher says syllables in a chain.
- Student(s) says and writes imaginary letters in the air for each word.
- Student(s) reads the nonword from memory.
- Teacher asks student(s) to recall a specific letter by its order in the syllable.
- Teacher asks student(s) to say the letters backwards.
- Teacher manipulates letters and student(s) reads the new word.

Once Buzz can *fairly easily* do simple syllable imaging, I extend him into complex syllable imaging, and the first move might be using the Syllable Board. Though, if I think his imagery is strong enough, I'll continue having him image in the air. In other words, I can get out the Syllable Board for the move into complex syllables, or I can simply have him go right from the above lesson into imaging complex syllables in the air. It is my choice based on his performance, and even if I don't do the sequencing board right now, I can always use it as a means of changing the task slightly, to keep interest and energy in the lesson, while still stimulating symbol imagery.

The following lesson takes Buzz into complex syllables. The symbol imagery exercises and error handling are the same as previous lessons, only just the complexity of the task has changed. Now, I may not have Buzz write the letters in the air each time, instead I might just have him tell me the letters he visualizes. By beginning to assume imagery, the lessons move more quickly and, I can always have him write a few in the air just to be sure he is still imaging.

SAMPLE LESSON

Imaging and Air-Writing at the Complex Syllable Level (Whole to Parts)

The Set

Nanci: *"Let's do some more word imagery practice, and this time we'll see if we can get into four and maybe even five letters.*

Buzz: "Yikes."

Nanci: *"You'll do great. This is just like what we have been doing up to now—sometimes you'll say the letters backwards, sometimes I'll ask you for a certain letter, and sometimes I'll change the letters and have you read the word to me. It's easy!"*

Buzz: "Mm." (Something between a groan and a grunt.)

"Sometimes you'll say the letters backwards... sometimes I'll ask you for a certain letter... sometimes I'll change the letters and have you read the word to me."

Lesson

Nanci: *"What letters do you see when I say the word, si. Say the word back to me, write it in the air…and, as usual, say the letters as you write!"*

Buzz: *"Si…***S-I***.*"* (He writes in the air saying each letter name.)

Nanci: *"Great. Change si to spi.*

Buzz: *"Spi…Spi…*Add a **P**…**S-P-I**.*"* (He says and writes the letters in the air.) "Do you want me to tell you what it says?"

Nanci: *"Sure."*

Buzz: *"Spi!"*

Nanci: *"Great. What's the second letter you see?"*

Buzz: "**P**."

Nanci: *"Great. Change spi to sti."*

Buzz: *"Sti…Sti…*Change the **P** to a **T**…**S-T-I**." (He says and writes the letters in the air.)

Nanci: *"Great. Now what's the second letter you see?"*

Buzz: "**T**."

Nanci: *"Right. Tell me the letters you see, backwards."*

Buzz: "Easy! **I-T-S**. (Saying each letter, hand up in the air touching the spot where they are in his imagination, but *not* writing the letters.)

Nanci: *"Yes. Yes. Let's keep going. Change sti to sli."*

Buzz: "Easy. The **T** changes to an **L**. *Sli.*"

Nanci: *"See I told you this was easy. Now what's the second letter you see?"*

Buzz: "**L**."

Nanci: *"Tell me all the letters you see, going from front to back.*

If using the ADD Program: "Say it after me to really feel the sounds in your mouth."

If not using the ADD Program, "Say it slowly to hear, feel, and image each letter."

Buzz: "**S-L-I**."

Nanci: *"Right. Here's another one. Change sli to sla."*

Buzz: "Easy again. The **I** changes to an **A**. *Sla*."

Nanci: *"Right. Backwards!'*

Buzz: "**A-L-S**."

Nanci: *"And what does the word say?"*

Buzz: "*Sla.*"

Nanci: *"Did you notice I didn't always have you write the letters in the air? Well, that's because I think you really can see these letters in your imagination so you don't always need to write them in the air anymore. Sometimes we'll do it just for fun, just to be sure you're still visualizing them.*

Buzz: "I really can see them. Are we going to try more letters?"

Nanci: *"Ohhhh, yessss! Ready? Change sla to slan."*

Buzz: "*Slan*…Add an **N**! **S-L-A-N**." (He says and writes the letters in the air.)

Nanci: *"See I told you this was easy. Now what's the second letter you see?"*

Buzz: "**L**."

Nanci: *"Tell me all the letters you see, backwards.*

Buzz: "**N-A-L-S**."

Nanci: *"Great. See it and say it!"*

Buzz: "*Slan.*"

Nanci: *"Oh, good…good…good. Take out the **S** and put in a **P**, now see it and say it."*

Buzz: "*Plan*. **P-L-A-N**. Hah! Real word."

Nanci: *"Yup! See how easy this is? Let's keep going. Change plan to plap."*

Buzz: "The **N** changes to a **P**. *Plap*."

Student doesn't always have to air-write each pattern.

Nanci: *"Great. Third letter?"*

Buzz: "**A**." (Eyes up visualizing.)

Nanci: *"Yes! Now, write that in the air…please…so, I'll be sure you're seeing it!*

Buzz: "**P-L-A-P**, *plap*." (Saying and writing in the air.)

Nanci: *"Excellent. Let's go to five letters. See if you can tell where the new letter comes in. Change plap to plasp."*

"Change plap to plasp"

Buzz: *"Plasp. Plasp.* (Eyes up.) Add an **S** after the **A**, right before the **P**! **P-L-A-S-P**." (He says and writes.)

Nanci: *"Great. Second letter you see?"*

Buzz: "**L**."

Nanci: *"Fourth letter you see?"*

Buzz: "Hmmm. (Eyes up, hand silently counting the letters in the air.) **S**."

Nanci: *"Excellent! Backwards, please.*

Buzz: "Mm. **P-S-A-L-P**."

Nanci: *"Yippee! You're really getting this! Write it in the air please, and see it and say it."*

Buzz: "*Plasp*!" (Writing the letters in the air first.)

Nanci: *"Excellent. Let's change a few more and then quit. Change plasp to plamp."*

Buzz: "*Plamp*. Change the **S** to an **M**. **P-L-A-M-P**." (He doesn't write, he only images.)

Nanci: *"Great. Fourth letter?*

Buzz: "**M**."

Nanci: *"Excellent. Change plamp to pramp."*

Buzz:	*"Pramp.* Easy. Change the **L** to an **R**." (He doesn't write, he doesn't spell out each letter, he only images.)
Nanci:	*"Change the **P** to a **T** and what does it say?"*
Buzz:	(Eyes up.) *"Tramp!"*
Nanci:	*"Oh. You're so good! Very soon I'm going to show you how to use this to study your spelling words, and how to use it to help you memorize words to make reading easier and faster. We'll have fun…won't we!"*

Lesson Summary:

Imaging and Air-Writing at the Complex Syllable Level (Whole to Parts)

- Teacher says syllables in a chain.
- Student(s) says and *sometimes* writes in the air, beginning to only imagine the letters, and thus hastening the lesson.
- Use the phrase "see and say."
- Teacher randomly does the *symbol imagery exercises*:

    —Student(s) sees and says the word from memory.

    —Student(s) recalls a specific letter by its order in the syllable.

    —Student(s) says the letters backwards.

    —Student(s) sees and says the word after teacher manipulates the letters.

As Buzz's symbol imagery has improved for hearing the word and imaging the letters (imaging the parts from the whole), I now shift the task slightly and have him hear the letters and image the word (imaging the whole from the parts). This lesson is at the complex syllable level, but I could have easily started it at the simple syllable level. It is another way to exercise the symbol imagery part of his sensory system.

	SAMPLE LESSON

Imaging and Air-Writing at the Complex Syllable Level (Parts to Whole)

The Set

Parts to whole:
Teacher says each letter,
student images the word.

Nanci: *"You have gotten good at imaging words when I say letters, now let's keep exercising that imaging part of your brain and change the task just a little bit. This time I'll say letters and you image the word. Get it?"*

Buzz: "Got it."

Nanci: *"Good."*

Lesson

Nanci: *"Here we go. What word do you see when I say the letters **F-L-A-P**?"*

"What word do you see when I say the letters **F-L-A-P**?"

Buzz: "**F-L-A-P**." (Saying and writing each letter in the air.) "*Flap*! Like *flap* your wings."

Nanci: *"Right. A real word, flap. Flap your wings and fly away from here! Just kidding. Now, I'll change one letter and you see if you can imagine the word. Remember to say and write the letters to help you get the image."*

Buzz: "Got it...and, I don't want to fly away anyhow..."

Nanci: *"It would be fun if we could, but we can't, so let's fly in our imagination. Fly these letters in—change **F-L-A-P** to **F-L-E-A-P**. What does the word say?"*

Buzz: (Saying and writing **F-L-E-A-P** in the air.) "*Fleap*."

Nanci: *"Right, and ..."*

115

Buzz: "If you took off the letter **F**, it would say *leap!*"

Continue to reinforce spelling patterns.

Nanci: *"Right, right. Good on you! Now change to F-L-A-P-E. See it and say it!"*

Buzz: (Saying and writing **F-L-A-P-E** in the air.) "Hmmm. **E** on the end...*Flape!*"

Nanci: *"Right. What's the fourth letter you see?"*

Buzz: "**P**."

Nanci: *"Right, again. Backwards!"*

Buzz: "**E-P-A-L-F**...*flape.*"

Nanci: *"I can't lose you! Change to F-L-A-C-E. See it and say it!"*

Buzz: "*Flace.*" (Not stopping this time to say and write the letters in the air, and recognizing the c rule of saying /s/ when followed by an e!)

"Change to F-L-A-C-E. See it and say it!"

Nanci: *"Right, What's the fourth letter you see?"*

Buzz: "**C**."

Nanci: *"Right. And what sound did it make and why?"*

Buzz: "It made the /s/ sound because it had an **E** after it. Isn't that right?"

Nanci: *"Absolutely right. Just checking, you know. Just checking that you didn't guess!"*

Buzz: "Hmmh." (Smiling with sort of a mutter.) "I don't have to do that anymore."

Lesson Summary:
Imaging and Air-Writing at the Complex Syllable Level (parts to whole)

- Teacher says *letters* for a nonword.
- Student(s) says letters and (*sometimes*) writes in the air, saying word by bringing parts to whole.
- *Symbol imagery exercises*:
  —Student(s) sees and says the word from memory.
  —Student(s) recalls a specific letter by its order in the syllable.
  —Student(s) says the letters backwards.
  —Student(s) sees and says the word after teacher manipulates the letters.
- Use English rules and expectancies to teach *memory* for how words are spelled.

Practice and Pacing

Practice and pacing is easy if these concepts are kept in mind: 1) concern for lesson energy, 2) monitoring task levels, 3) overlapping steps, and 4) a goal of self-correction and quasi-automaticity.

Keep a watchful eye on the energy of the lesson. I have seen clinically competent teachers always question to the response, choose good patterns, do the right exercises, but not monitor the energy of the lesson. They don't seem to notice that students are barely able to stand the boredom, either because the lesson is too long or the teacher is passive and doesn't exude positive energy. I've tried to demonstrate throughout these sample lessons, positive energy and humor with Buzz. Having fun is a very important part of teaching, some light-heartedness to involve the student more emotionally. Clinically good instruction may not achieve as much gain as possible because the instructor was passive, no connection to the student, no fun, no silliness, no spark. Whereas, not-so-good instructing techniques may make superior progress, seeming to make up for the lack of precise questioning or instructional quality with an active personality, an almost noticeable connection to the students. Practice time can take as long as the lesson has energy, varying between twenty minutes to four hours, depending on the variety of tasks.

Monitoring the level of the task means moving through simple patterns on to complex, but remember to start complex imaging at the VCC and CCV level, rather than catapulting right into CCVCC. When to move from one level to the next depends on the processing skills of the student(s), usually eighty percent competency.

Overlapping steps has been discussed before, but remains a very important concept for good pacing. In developing imagery for sequencing sounds in syllables, two steps can be overlapped: the Syllable Board and air-writing with a chain. The Syllable Board provides the student with more concreteness than just writing in the air, so you may want to use it for awhile, but eventually you want the student imaging without even having to air-write each pattern.

The sensory system has dominos that are prerequisites for independence. The sensory-input (imagery) domino comes before the monitoring (hold and compare) domino, and the self-correction domino comes before the independence domino. Noting self-correcting behaviors provides important diagnostic information for pacing, as does noting when the student begins to demonstrate rapid responses—automaticity—the final goal. Quasi-automaticity is non-slow responses. Not necessarily *fast* responses, but accurate and not painfully slow. As the student is being paced from one step to the next, full automaticity (mastery) is not expected, but quasi-automaticity is desired.

Summary

Symbol imagery stimulation through <u>Imaging and Air-Writing with a Chain</u> continues to consciously develop the hold and compare process necessary for monitoring and self-correction—heading toward independence. By using patterns in a chain, the student is forced to hold an old pattern and compare it with a new—replicating what the sensory system does when processing language. When comfortable with receiving the word and imaging the letters (whole to parts), the hold and compare task is gently extended to receiving the letters and imaging the word (parts to whole).

The goal of *Seeing Stars* is to develop the students' ability to image without having to write the letters in the air, in preparation for the actual experience of processing language quickly and accurately. With this is mind, the student begins to just see and say the letters or word, rather than writing in the air for every change. This hastens the lesson, allowing for more symbol imagery within a given period of time.

Summary: Step 5

Imaging & Sequencing Syllables: Air-Writing *with* a Chain

> **Goal:** To develop symbol imagery for sounds within words from the simple through complex level, and teach visual memory for regularly irregular spelling patterns.

1. Student writes imaginary letters in the air.

2. A chain of syllables is presented to develop the hold and compare process.

3. The stimulation moves from simple to complex syllables.

4. Use common irregularities, such as "final e" and "two vowels go walking" rule, tch, dge, etc.

5. Stimulation starts with whole to parts, with teacher saying word and student imaging letters.

6. Stimulation moves to parts to whole, with teacher saying letters and student imaging word.

7. Use the phrase "see it and say it" when having students decode from imagery.

8. Do symbol imagery exercises:

- DECODE: Student reads the syllable from the imaged pattern (memory).
- IDENTIFY: Student identifies a specific letter from the imaged pattern.
- BACKWARDS: Student says the letters backwards from the imaged pattern.
- MANIPULATE: Student reads the syllable from imagery, after letters are manipulated.

Lesson Summary

- Teacher says syllables or letters in a chain, extending into CCVCC.

- Student(s) says and sometimes writes in the air, beginning to only imagine the letters, and thus hastening the lesson.

- Teacher randomly does the symbol imagery exercises:

  —Student(s) sees and says the word from memory.

  —Student(s) recalls a specific letter by its order in the syllable.

  —Student(s) says the letters backwards.

  —Student(s) sees and says the word after teacher manipulates the letters.

- Use English rules and expectancies to teach memory for how words

---

Group Instruction

Small or large group instruction does not require changing the stimulation for the imaging and air-writing step. Each student does symbol imagery exercises or students are called on randomly for answers, using the thumbs up or down involvement. Small groups of students often verbalize the answer in unison. All in all, easy and fun.

Imaging & Sequencing Syllables:
Air-Writing *without* a Chain

This last step of imaging and sequencing sounds in syllables extends the imaging process to a variety of words, either from whole to parts or from parts to whole. No more chains. The sound sequencing stimulation through imagery has moved from the syllable board, to a chain, and now to no chain. Each word changes and thus has to be imaged from scratch without the support of a previous pattern. The hold and compare stimulation can be developed receptively with the teacher miscalling the imaged stimulus and the student noting the error. This sets the student up for judging his or her own errors, thus specifically practicing the monitoring task.

Here is Buzz at the complex level, doing syllable imaging without a chain, and moving in and out of receiving a word to receiving letters. His feathers are fluffing out, his wings mending.

| SAMPLE LESSON |

Imaging and Air-Writing without a Chain (Whole to Parts and Parts to Whole)

Words to letters and letters to words.

The Set

Nanci: *"Well, you are so good at imaging letters in words, this time we'll add just a little bit more fun to the task. Instead of just changing one letter at a time, I'll give you a new word each time."*

Buzz: "A bunch of new letters each time? A whole new word each time?"

No chains. Each stimulus is a new word.

Nanci: *"Yup. Just like in the real world of reading and spelling…and you'll do great."*

Buzz: "Mm." (The groan/grunt.)

"What letters do you see when I say the word, *sep.* Say the word back to me…and say the letters you visualize!"

Teach flexibility in spelling patterns.

Lesson

Nanci: *"What letters do you see when I say the word, sep. Say the word back to me, write it in the air…and, as usual, say the letters as you write!"*

Buzz: "*Sep…***S-E-P**." (He writes in the air saying each letter name.)

Nanci: *"Great. Now what letters do you see when I say, kif?"*

Buzz: "*Kif…***K-I-F**. Want me to do it backwards?"

Nanci: *"Hot shot. Sure, I was going to ask you anyhow!"*

Buzz: "**F-I-K**, *kif.*"

Nanci: *"Great. I told you this was easy. What's the last letter you see?"*

Buzz: "**F**."

Nanci: *"Great. Now do preep."*

Buzz: "Preep is **P-R-E-E-P**. Oh, wait and it also could be **E-A** instead of **E-E**. Right?"

Nanci: *"Absolutely. And, if you hadn't told me that I would have asked you what else could say the sound of **E** because I want you to be flexible in spelling, because you have to be able to think of alternatives in order to spell accurately. As you know, all words don't play fair, aren't written like they sound."*

Buzz: "That's for sure. I think imaging may help me remember those parts that don't play fair."

Nanci: *"Yes. You'll be able to remember the irregularities better for both spelling and reading. For reading, you'll be able to memorize words easily so you won't have to sound-out so many or guess from the sentence. Get it?"*

"What's the fourth letter you see ?"

"Your brain was always able to do this. It was just waiting for someone to show it how... and give it practice."

Teacher miscues, student notes the error.

Buzz: "Got it! Let's do some more. I have a big test coming up, I think I'd better get as much practice as I can."

Nanci: *"Yes. Yes. Let's keep going. What do you see if I say F-L-E-S-H?"*

Buzz: "Hmmm. That's pretty easy. Real word. *Flesh.* Right?"

Nanci: *"Yup. I told you this was easy. Now what's the fourth letter you see?"*

Buzz: "**S**. And, I can do it backwards…**H-S-E-L-F**. Just so you know, when I have to say it to you backwards that really makes me visualize the word. Really. At first it was hard and now it's not. Amazing my brain has learned to do this."

Nanci: *"Your brain was always able to do this. It was just waiting for someone to show it how and give it practice. Let's do something fun for a moment. You be the teacher and I'll be the student. You tell me if I'm right or wrong, and how I'm wrong. If we visualize F-L-E-S-H, am I right if I read the word as fresh?"*

Buzz: "*Fresh?* No, you put an **R**, where the **L** is!"

Nanci: *"Hmm. What if I said F-L-E-S-H said flash. Am I right?"*

Buzz: "**F-L-E-S-H**. (Eyes looking up to image.) *Flash.* No. You put an **A** where the **E** is!"

Nanci: *"Excellent. If you can judge my errors, you'll be able to judge your errors, and you won't need me anymore. Isn't that great? You'll be independent."*

Buzz: "Hmmm. I think I see. I'll be able to fix words myself rather than have to ask the teacher or my mom if I'm right."

Nanci: *"Exactly."*

Buzz: "Hmmm."

Nanci: *"OK. Here's some more for you to image. Remember, I'll always give you the letters to see from front to back. I'll never give them to you backwards."*

*"See and say this word, **C-L-A-P-P-E-D**."*

Buzz: (Saying and writing the letters in the air for help). **C-L-A-P-P-E-D**. *Clapped*, like I clapped my hands."

Nanci: *"Correct. I know the end of that word sounds like /t/, but on real words we spell it with an **ED**. The **ED** just makes it the past tense—meaning it happened before, not now. Do you know why the two **P's** are there?"*

Buzz: "Sort of. Maybe you could tell me again."

Nanci: *"Sure. The two **P's** mean the vowel can't say it's name, it has to say it's sound."*

Buzz: Mm."

> "Remember, I'll always give you the letters to see from front to back. I'll never give them to you backwards."

I proceeded to explain to Buzz the doubling rule in English and we practiced more with it. We also used these lessons to practice visualizing *tch* in real words, *dge*, etc. Later in the week we got out his spelling words, imaged them, and Buzz got his first 100 on a spelling test. More importantly, he could still spell his words weeks later because they were in his long term memory. Spelling was becoming his friend, not his enemy, and equally significant, it was becoming something he didn't have to consciously think about; thus, he could get on with thinking about other things in life that did require conscious attention! He was beginning to flap his wings.

Lesson Summary:
*Imaging and Air-Writing **without** a Chain*

- Teacher says syllables or letters, without a chain—a new word each time.

- Student(s) says letters and (*sometimes*) writes in the air, saying word by bringing parts to whole or whole to parts.

- Use English rules and expectancies to teach *memory* for how words are spelled.

- Teacher miscalls the imaged word and student(s) judges and notes error.

- Do *symbol imagery exercises*:

    —Student(s) sees and says the word from memory.

    —Student(s) recalls a specific letter by its order in the syllable.

    —Student(s) says the letters backwards.

    —Student(s) sees and says the word after teacher manipulates the letters.

Practice and Pacing

Pacing and practice at this step requires the same attention to lesson energy, appropriate movement through the task levels, overlapping of steps, and attention to the quickness of the students response. The symbol imagery exercises are now devoting more attention to regularly irregular patterns, and those should be presented carefully without overloading the student and ultimately frustrating him or her. Present a few irregularities, getting the student to grasp them with about eighty percent accuracy and then add a few more.

Students should get comfortable with the more common irregularities or spelling patterns before overwhelming them with the quirks of English. Most words do play fair, and the ones that don't are usually only irregular in one spot, sometimes two. Very rarely will the whole word be irregular but those are the ones you and I remember through symbol imagery!

Summary

This air-writing activity (whole/parts and parts/whole) continues to stimulate symbol imagery, but without the support of a chain; thus, evolving more fully toward the hold and compare process necessary for the real world of reading and spelling.

With miscalling consciously developing the monitoring domino, and attention to spelling patterns, this step is the final preparation before application of symbol imagery to sight words, spelling, and contextual reading.

Summary:
Step 6

Imaging & Sequencing Syllables: Air-Writing *without* a Chain

Goal: To develop symbol imagery for sounds/letters within words from the simple through complex level, and teach visual memory for regularly irregular spelling patterns.

1. Teacher says syllables or letters without a chain, a new word each time.

2. Student writes imaginary letters in the air.

3. The stimulation moves from simple to complex syllables.

4. From word to word all the sounds and letters change, no chaining.

5. Miscalling stimulates the hold and compare process.

6. Use common spelling irregularities.

7. Stimulation is mixed between whole to parts and parts to whole (word to letters or letters to word).

8. Do symbol imagery exercises:

   - DECODE: Student reads the syllable from the imaged pattern (memory).
   - IDENTIFY: Student identifies a specific letter from the imaged pattern.
   - BACKWARDS: Student says the letters backwards from the imaged pattern.
   - MANIPULATE: Student reads the syllable from imagery, after letters are manipulated.

Lesson Summary

- Teacher says syllables or letters without a chain, a new word each time, extending into complex syllables.
- Student(s) sees and says and sometimes writes in the air.
- Teacher miscalls the imaged word and student(s) judges and notes error.
- Symbol imagery exercises:
  —Student(s) sees and says the word from memory.
  —Student(s) recalls a specific letter by its order in the syllable.
  —Student(s) says the letters backwards.
  —Student(s) sees and says the word after teacher manipulates the letters.
- More focus on teaching spelling expectancies for memory of common spelling patterns.

Group Instruction

As with the previous step, small or large group instruction does not require change. Each student is given a word or letters to write in the air and/or does symbol imagery exercises. Continue thumbs up or down to demonstrate attention to the response. The miscalling activity is fun with students taking turns correcting the teacher's error. Perfect for working on vocabulary, sight words, spelling, terms, etc.

Imaging Sight Words

15

With the symbol imagery base developed, or *developing* as we overlap steps of *Seeing Stars*, the next logical step in this stimulation is to apply symbol imagery to the establishment of a sight word base for reading. The Visual Circle is one of the critical circles in literacy development and a critical aspect for an integrated approach to reading. With phonological processing developed, or developing, it is the Visual Circle's moment.

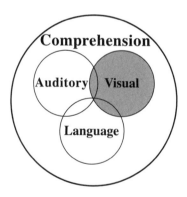

As was discussed in Chapter Five, phonological processing does not make a reader, it is the integration of good word attack skills with sight words, with context, with vocabulary, and with comprehension that makes a *reader*. Reading is getting meaning. Reading too slowly because numerous words have to be phonetically processed, may interrupt meaning. Furthermore, slow decoding often invites guessing from context, which may or may not be correct and thus may or may not give the student the author's intended imagery. A well developed sight vocabulary increases the pace of contextual reading, but instant word recognition requires that the underlying sensory-cognitive processes of phonemic awareness and symbol imagery be in tact.

Blossoming symbol imagery now allows me to move Buzz into sight words, expanding his memorized base, and developing his Visual Circle. Using the most common word lists, such as the Fry (see Appendix), I begin the stimulation with symbol imagery and *repetitive exposure*. I have observed teachers and clinicians "teaching sight words" by showing words to a student once or twice a day, or sending them home to be read after dinner or on the way to school. Even with well developed symbol imagery, students need to see words more than a few times to memorize them, especially since they are usually working on many words at the same time. Instant recognition is the goal for sight words, not phonetic processing, and instant recognition requires concentrated, consistent exposure.

As we move into an era in education where we value phonetic processing, we must not abandon sight word instruction, nor think that sight words are developed because they can be self-corrected or phonetically processed "sort of fast." Sight words have to be *fast*! Instant recognition! No hesitation! No spit and grunt! Without them, Buzz is going to slowly sound words out when he gets back on the page. And frustrated, he may revert back to guessing at both long and short words in his effort to read fluently. He'll still be in trouble, because though one of the reading circles is intact (Auditory), the other circles aren't. Development in one circle does not guarantee development in all. We must not make this mistake again, whether from the linguist, look-say, or psycho-linguist camp. We must have an integrated approach to teaching reading. Too many children have dropped out of the V formation. There are too many Buzzes.

In teaching sight words, first determine which words the student already recognizes instantly by checking through a list of the most commonly read words. (If working with young children, who are reading for the first time, this doesn't apply, and you would move to putting words on cards.) Words that are self-corrected, somewhat slow, or very slow are to be put on cards for instant recognition, and then categorized into slow, medium, and fast piles named by the student. Once specific words are captured and categorized into piles, they are symbol imaged and reinforced repetitively.

Steps to develop sight words for the Visual Circle:

1. *Capture and Categorize*
   - Use a most commonly read list, such as Fry.
   - Capture the words not recognized immediately.
   - Put slow words on cards in lower case, bold letters.
   - Categorize the words into slow, medium, and fast piles.
2. *Symbol image*
   - Do symbol imagery exercises with words to place them in visual memory.
3. *Reinforce*
   - Reinforce repetitively, moving words from slow to fast piles.

Here is Buzz bridging into sight words and learning about the Venn diagram (the Reading Circles) to note where he is in the gestalt of reading and why he is going to work on this next step with me.

SAMPLE LESSON

Sight Words: Capture and Categorize

The Set

Nanci: *"It's time to begin sight words, and improve this circle. (I show Buzz the Venn diagram of the Reading Circles, focusing on the Visual Circle.)*

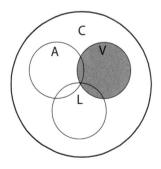

"This circle represents knowing words instantly, being able to recognize them really, really fast, which means remembering them, not having to sound them out. When you can do that, reading gets much, much easier and quicker."

"This circle represents knowing words instantly, being able to recognize them really, really fast,

which means remembering them, not having to sound them out. When you can do that, reading gets much, much easier and quicker."

Buzz: "I know some words fast."

Nanci: *"I know you do. In fact, let's find out which ones you know really fast and which ones you don't. And, the ones you don't, we'll put on cards and have that new part of your brain—imaging— help you remember them. That way we can make this circle, bigger and bigger. (I show him how we will get the visual circle bigger and bigger.)*

Buzz: "OK. I'm ready."

Lesson

Nanci: *"Here's a list of words and we'll just go down and see which ones are fast and which are slow. (Using two cards together, I flash a word with the cards by moving the bottom card down to expose the word and then quickly covering it with the top card.)*

Buzz: *"And, the, is, up..."* then a pause..."*say."*

Nanci: *"We'll put the word **say** on a card, because although you can read it, we want it to be instant. Really fast!"*

Though Buzz read some words like *the, and, will, was,* instantly, he was quite slow at words like *because, many, know, could, begin.* Note, that it wasn't just phonetically inconsistent words that he couldn't recognize instantly, it was also longer words that were phonetically consistent. He simply had not possessed the symbol imagery (visual memory) necessary for learning sight words, regular or irregular. His slow reading was more evident with irregular words because the phonetic processing he could do, spit and grunt though it was, was thwarted by the irregular nature of common words in English. Also, his Visual

- Capture slow words
- Put slow words on cards
- Catagorize words into slow, medium, & fast piles

He simply had not possessed the symbol imagery (visual memory) necessary for learning sight words, regular or irregular.

Circle might have seemed to be more developed than it actually was because with short, play fair words he could put the sounds in the right place fast enough to make it seem that he recognized them rather than phonetically processed them.

Nanci: *"So, let's keep going and put the slow words on cards."*

Buzz: "OK. But, I think we're going to have quite a few cards."

Nanci: *"That's OK, we'll just move the cards from a slow pile, to a medium pile, to your fast pile. It will be like a game. We'll try to see how big we can get your fast pile. In fact, you can even name the slow, medium, and fast piles. Like "turtles" for the slow pile, etc."*

Buzz: "OK. Like the medium pile can be "Dogs" because they're kind of slow, and the fast pile can be "Jets.""

Nanci: *"Fine with me. You can name them anything you want!"*

We did more words, until it seemed we had about twenty to go on cards. Then I created his sight word cards by writing each word on a 3X5 card—carefully writing in lower case letters and a moderately heavy black pen to help his symbol imagery. Getting a plastic box and cardboard dividers to hold the 3X5 index cards we began sorting his words into the categories of Turtles, Dogs, and Jets.

Nanci: *"Now that we have quite a few on cards—and notice how carefully I wrote them so you could image them for your memory system—let's begin to sort them for Turtles, Dogs, and Jets."*

Buzz: "How do we know the Turtles from the Dogs?"

Write captured sight words on 3X5 cards.

Name the slow, medium, and fast categories.

Nanci: *"Easy. When they are really, really slow, they are your Turtles. When they are only somewhat slow, they are your Dogs. And, when they are really, really, really fast, they are your Jets. Even if you correct yourself they can't be Jets because your Jets have to be fast, really fast, to help you read in books better."*

Buzz: "Whew. That would be good. I hate reading because I have to do that all the time…and, and sometimes I can't do it very fast."

Nanci: *"I know."*

Buzz: "I try because I want to read like everyone else, but I'm slow. It takes me so long that I start to guess…and them I'm sometimes wrong. (Thoughtful.) Is this really going to help?"

Nanci: *"Yes. We're just going to build up that Visual Circle I showed you, and get a whole bunch of words to be really, really fast. The more words you get to the Jet pile, the bigger that Visual Circle will be! And, then reading will be so much easier."*

Buzz: "OK. Am I going to use the imaging I learned to do?"

Nanci: *"That's the next thing we're going to do with these words! First, let's get them in their piles of Turtles, Dogs, and Jets. Remember, it really doesn't matter what pile they start in, because the game is to move them into the Jets."*

"First, let's get them in their piles of Turtles, Dogs, and Jets. Remember, it really doesn't matter what pile they start in, because the game is to move them into the Jets."

Showing Buzz each word, *I* decide which pile they go in. Naturally, his Turtle pile is the biggest, with a few Dogs, and no Jets! In the days to come, we *capture and categorize* more and more words, while he is moving his Turtles into Jets with symbol imagery.

Lesson Summary:
Sight Words and Categorize

- Check student(s) through a list of sight words, by flashing each word.
- Put words not recognized *immediately* on 3X5 cards.
- Write the word in lower case letters with a moderately heavy black pen.
- *Name* the slow, medium, and fast piles of cards.
- *Sort* the words into slow, medium, and fast piles.
- Put sight words in plastic box with dividers to note slow, medium, fast categories.
- Continually collect more words by repeating the process of *capturing and categorizing*.

Previous to knowing how to develop symbol imagery, the next step I might have done with Buzz was just *practice*. With no other options, we would have gone over and over the words, hoping they would somehow stick; thus, we would be practicing a task without the underlying sensory-cognitive function necessary for storage and retrieval. This can be compared to what educators did, and still do, in teaching "phonics." Not knowing *how* to develop phonemic awareness, students have often practiced workbook pages without possessing the necessary underlying sensory-cognitive function. In both cases, the Auditory and Visual Circles may remain underdeveloped, and thus not fulfilling their critical role in reading.

Having captured and categorized the words, Buzz will use symbol imagery to place the sight words in memory.

Expanding the visual circle:
"Now that we have your words sorted into piles, we'll start using that imagery part of your brain to help you memorize them."

"This is just like what we've been doing...what's the third letter you see?"

SAMPLE LESSON

"Symbol Imaging" Exercises for Sight Words

The Set

Nanci: *"Now that we have your words sorted into piles, we'll start using that imagery part of your brain to help you memorize them. Just like I told you, we're going to build up that Visual Circle."*

Buzz: "OK."

Nanci: *"I'm going to show you one of your Turtle words to read, and then I'll take it away. After I take it away, I want you to see it and say it, then tell me the letters you saw.*

Buzz: "OK. I'm ready."

Lesson

Nanci: *"I'm just going to start with about ten Turtle words. Here's the first one. (I hold up his word* **afraid***. What does that say?"*

Buzz: "Hmmm.../a/...(Sounding it out first as /a/–f-r-ae-d, with the /a/ sound for the first letter, he says it twice like that until finally his oral vocabulary converts the sounds.) Oh. *Afraid.*"

Nanci: *"Right. That's the word* **afraid***. (Taking the card away.) See it in your imagination, say it, and tell me its letters."*

Buzz: "*Afraid.* **A–F–R–A–I–D**." (Saying and writing the letters, without having to be asked, so I assumed he needed to air-write for support.)

Nanci: *"Great. See, this is just like what we've been doing. What is the third letter you see?"*

Buzz: "**R**." (Eyes up, small hand up counting off the letters he is imaging.)

Nanci: *"Right. How about the fifth letter you see?"*

Buzz: "**I**!"

Nanci: *"Right! Now say the letters again to me."*

Buzz: "**A-F-R-A-I-D**." (Not writing the letters in the air, apparently because he didn't need to.)

Nanci: *"Make up a sentence for me, using that word; and then tell me the letters you see again."*

Buzz: "Hmmm. I used to be afraid of the dark. **A-F-R-A-I-D**."

Nanci: *"Great. Take a look at it on this card again, tell me again what it says, and then let's do some more of your words." (I show him the **afraid** card again.)*

Buzz: "*Afraid.*"

We practiced a few more, and after each word was "symbol imaged," he read it along with the ones he had imaged previously.

Irregular Words:

The next word we did was irregular. The symbol imagery exercises were the same with one modification: Buzz notes the irregularity, particularly placing that part in memory.

Nanci: *"Here's the next word. (I hold up the card **what**). Know what this word is?"*

Buzz: "Wh-/a/-t." (Saying /a/ for the letter **a**, just as he would think.) "Wh-/a/-t...oh, this is the word *what*. Right?"

> Irregular words are practiced but, Buzz notes the irregularity, particularly placing that part in memory.

Nanci: *"Yes, and if you were reading it in a sentence the words around it might help you get it, but having to read sentences over a few times to get a word takes a lot of time. That's why we want these words to get to your Jet pile.*

*"So, in the word **what**, what part doesn't play fair? What part doesn't sound like it looks?"*

Buzz: "The letter **a** doesn't say what it should say!"

Nanci: *"Right. You'll have to just remember it says **what**, but most of the word plays fair, so that will help you.*

"Let's image it. Take a look at the card again, and then after I take it away see it and say it, then give me the letters."

Buzz: *"What.* **W-H-A-T**.*"*

Nanci: *"Great. What is the third letter you see."*

Buzz: "That **A**."

Nanci: *"Right! Say the word and the letters again."*

Buzz: *"What.* **W-H-A-T**.*"*

Nanci: *"Letters again!"*

Buzz: **"W-H-A-T**." (Hand up tracking the letters, not writing them.)

Nanci: *"Great. Let me show you the word card again and you say it. Then we'll put it with the other ones we've imaged today and read each of them again."*

**Very irregular words:
"Let me tell you this word because most of it doesn't play fair. "**

Very Irregular Words:

Here is what to do with very irregular words, of which there are very few.

Nanci: *"Here's the next word. (I hold up the card **enough**). Know what this word is?"*

Buzz: "/e/-n-ou-g-h." (Trying to say each sound, puzzled because nothing in his oral vocabulary matches it.)

Nanci: *"Let me just tell you this word because most of it doesn't play fair, and I don't want you to struggle and struggle for no reason. It says **enough**."*

Buzz: "Oh, yeah."

Nanci: *"Take a look at it closely, then I'll take it away and we'll image it just like all the others we've done. Nothing different, just more to remember! But, this time be sure and say and write the letters in the air."*

"What are the last two letters you see?"

Buzz: "*Enough.* **E-N-O-U-G-H**." (Saying and writing in the air.)

Nanci: *"What are the last two letters you see?"*

Buzz: "Hmmm…**G-H**, but they sound like /f/."

Nanci: *"Yup. And, there isn't anything you or I can do about it, except remember them. And, once you remember them you won't ever have to think about it anymore. You'll be able to read and spell the word just as easily as you read and spell your own name.*

*What are all the letters you see for **enough**?"*

Buzz: "**E-N-O-U-G-H**. (Hand up, not writing them but marking them as he goes.)

Nanci: *"Great. Your Visual Circle is going to get bigger and bigger! Look at the card again and tell me what it says."* (I show him the card **enough** again.)

Buzz: "*Enough.* I think I've had enough!"

Nanci: *"Good sentence…"*

> **Lesson Summary:**
> *"Symbol Imaging" Exercises for Sight Words*
>
> - Use symbol imagery exercises to place categorized words into memory.
> - Student(s) sees and says a sight word and *sometimes* writes in the air.
> - Symbol imagery exercises:
>   —Student(s) sees and says the word from memory.
>   —Student(s) recalls a specific letter by its order in the syllable.
>   —Student(s) says the letters backwards.
>   —Student(s) sees and says the word after teacher manipulates the letters.

Phonetic Markings on Sight Word Cards:
To Do or Not to Do?

Most words in English are phonetically consistent, or reasonably so. Given good phonemic awareness, the words can be decoded; and, given good concept imagery, vocabulary can be extended and meaning derived; and, given good symbol imagery, those same words will automatically be placed in a memorized sight vocabulary, not to be worried about again. All of this happens automatically and painlessly for the student with the underlying sensory-cognitive processes necessary to be a good reader. But, the student having difficulty with phonetic processing and symbol imagery finds the irregular nature of some common English words an added nail in the coffin. Placing those irregular words into memory becomes a formidable task.

As a student becomes able to phonetically process words *overlapping* to memorizing sight words can be frustrating. The newly developed auditory system is now keenly aware of the phonetic irregularities of some English words, especially in the first two hundred common words. Thus, a plan for learning them is important at this stage in Buzz's flight plan.

A few irregular sight words may be marked with phonetic representations on the bottom right corner in a very light pencil to give him some assistance in learning the word. But, working on sight words is building the Visual Circle, not the Auditory Circle, and a minimal number of cards should be marked as it imprints the wrong visual pattern in the visual memory system, interrupting spelling and the building of the Visual Circle. Though the phonetic markings *will* help Buzz continue to build phonetic processing and self-correction, they *will not* help him quickly increase his sight word base and the Visual Circle. Seeing the word *many* written as "meny" interrupts the visual pattern of the word *many* and is not necessary since sounding it out as m/a/ny is very close to what it really does sound like. Symbol imagery is a quicker, more efficient way to place the word in the memory system than a phonetic representation, and doesn't disturb the visual pattern, and thus doesn't disturb spelling.

Therefore, rather than marking the phonetic pattern on many sight word cards, take the time to have the student create a sentence with you about the meaning of the word, and then write that on the back of the card. When the student is learning the word, reading the sentence on the back of the card gives him or her practice with the sight word (as well as practice imaging symbols and concepts) and also practice reading the additional words in the sentence.

With that caution in mind, there are a few words that may need to be phonetically marked initially to help the student decode the word. But the phonetic representation should be erased as soon as possible, and only shown when the student is completely stuck when decoding it. For example, if I have marked "ee-nuf" on the bottom right corner of the sight word *enough*, when I practice that word with Buzz I am going to keep the phonetic representation covered up and see if he can say the word first. If he becomes frustrated, I will uncover it, let him sound it out, and then cover it again so that he *sees* the correct pattern of the word, *enough* and not the incorrect pattern *ee-nuf*!

Repetitive Reinforcement of Sight Words

Once words are analyzed with symbol imagery exercises, they need to be practiced until recognized immediately, automatically. This requires more than just flashing them over and over, one after the other.

One of the most important aspects in developing the Visual Circle is *repetitive practice* where the sight words are seen *many* times throughout the reinforcement.

Since repetitive practice can be boring, there are creative techniques to challenge the student and add fun to the practice. Two techniques to keep the lessons fun while also providing repetition are "Wake up and Put to Sleep" and "Read and Step," the latter more effective with children than adults.

Here is Buzz learning his sight words with repetition. Placing the three piles of words on the table, with the slowest pile to the right of him, he is challenged to get his words moved from the slow to the medium pile, then to the fast pile. He will *see* his Dogs and Jets grow.

SAMPLE LESSON

Repetitive Reinforcement of Sight Words

"Wake up and Put to Sleep"

Sight word reinforcement: "Wake-up and put to sleep"

The Set

Nanci: *"Let's practice these words and get them moved over to the Jets. (Placing all three piles of sight words in front of him.) We'll take seven words from the Turtles, and walk up and down the row of words waking them up and putting them to sleep."*

Buzz: "OK. My Turtle pile is pretty big. (Squinting his eyes a little.)

Words form columns to go up and down like a ladder.

Nanci: *"I know. And, tomorrow maybe we'll take ten Turtles out instead of seven, or maybe even more. But today, to get used to this game, we'll start with seven.*

Lesson

"We'll start at the bottom, you touch the word, read it, then touch and read the next one—and up the ladder of words you'll go."

Nanci: *"Let's make the Turtle pile smaller. Here are seven we have imaged. Let's practice them by walking up and down. Here we go. We'll start at the bottom, you touch the word, read it, then touch and read the next one—and up the ladder of words you'll go."*

Buzz: "OK. That word is…be- - be - -kau- -s- …be- -kau-s…*because.*"

Nanci: *"Great. Touch and read the word again, altogether, before you go on.*

Buzz: "Because."

Nanci: *"Good job. Now touch and read the next word."*

Buzz: "This word is…m-/a/-n—ee, m-/a/-nee… oh, *many.*"

We continue the reinforcement, up the ladder, touching and reading the cards, and back down so each word has been read two times.

Nanci: *"You've gone up and down the ladder, now let's go back up it again and as you say the word turn it over and put it to sleep." (Back up Buzz went.)*

Buzz: "Be-kau…*because.* (Turning it over.) M/ a/…*many.*" (Turning it over.)

Now his decoding of *because* and *many* is a little faster because this is the third time he has read the words. He gets to the top of the ladder with each word now put to sleep.

Nanci: *"Great. ZZZZZZZZZZ (An imitation snore that makes him smile…despite himself.) Now come back down and wake them up."*

Buzz: "OK." (Starting at the top, he turns over a card, decodes it, much more quickly, does the next one, and the next one until he has them all turned over and decoded. He has now read each word four times.)

Nanci: *"Great. Now let's mix them up and see if you can still put them to sleep pretty quickly. They're very tired you know." (Smile again. I scramble them out of the sequence he became used to when he went up and down the ladder.)*

Continue the reinforcement, up the ladder, touching and reading the cards, and back down so each word has been read two times.

Starting at the top, he turns over a card, decodes it, much more quickly, does the next one, and the next one until he has them all turned over and decoded. He has now read each word four times.

Buzz: "Hmmm. *Many, before, again.*" (Starting at the bottom card, which just happened to be the word *many*. Now reading the words quite quickly, moving fairly rapidly toward the top, he put the words to sleep as he went.)

Nanci: *"Great. They're all asleep again, let me scramble them one more time, and you can go down the ladder and wake them up."* (Scrambling them, still turned over, asleep.)

Buzz: *"Again, because, many, before, where, them, they, were."* (Turning them over and quite rapidly decoding them. He has now, rather painlessly, read each word six times.)

Nanci: *"Lightening fast, aren't you. Try this. I'll scramble them one more time, and the ones you can read very quickly, we'll move to the Dogs. Then we'll check those a little later to see if they're still fast, and tomorrow if they're really fast, we'll move them to the Jets."*

(Scrambling them one last time. Buzz begins to touch and read them. This is the seventh time he has read each word.)

Buzz: *"Before, because, many, again, …"* (Each word he read quickly, we moved to the Dog pile, only two words stayed in the Turtles because he hesitated on them: *where* and *were*.)

Nanci: *"Great. You moved five words over, and now lets get five new words out of the Turtles, and we'll keep these two (where and were), so we have a total of seven. Just think of how many times you'll get to practice these two as we wake them up and put them to sleep. Very soon they'll be over in the Dogs too."*

As we repeat the stimulation with new words, the two that were somewhat slow may be read another

---

Sidenotes:

Turning them over and quite rapidly decoding them. He has now, rather painlessly, read each word six times.

Scrambling them one last time. Buzz begins to touch and read them. This is the seventh time he has read each word.

We'll bring out some more Turtles to keep at least seven in the reinforcement loop.

seven times. It is very likely they will move to the Dogs the next round, or even before we get through the stimulation, in which case, we'll bring out some more Turtles to keep at least seven in the reinforcement loop.

Buzz: "Yeah. I see what you mean. My Turtles are getting a little smaller…Let's do it again."

"Read and Step"

Nanci: *"This time let's practice your Dogs to get your Visual Circle bigger and bigger. Let's do something different. You can stand up, over there (about twelve feet away). I'll show you a word, you read it and take a step. If you say it pretty quickly, you can take a big step, if it takes you a long time, you can only take a small step."*

Buzz: "OK!" (Glad to be up and about, he goes over, little feet together perfectly, and waits for me to hold up one of his Dogs.)

Nanci: *"Here we go. (I hold up a word card, making sure Buzz can see from that distance!)*

Buzz: *"Because."*

Nanci: *"Excellent. Take a big step."*

Buzz: *"Many."*

Nanci: *"Excellent again. Take a step."*

Read and Step:
"I'll show you a word, you read it and take a step. If you say it pretty quickly, you can take a big step, if it takes you a long time, you can only take a small step."

We continue the "Read and Step" game across the room, back and forth. Sometimes he steps backwards as he reads, so he can get back to the start. Mixing them up, especially choosing the words that are still moderately slow, I have Buzz read them again.

In a few days, Buzz learned to instantly recognize over a hundred common sight words, was beginning to increase his fluency in contextual reading and, because of the imagery work (which is laced into the reinforcement sessions), his visual memory system was being prepared for spelling. Sometimes the stimulation was with the cards out in piles as described above, and sometimes it was just grabbing a pile of Turtles and flashing them to see how many he could get to his pile before they went to my pile (they went to my pile when he was too slow). However I chose to reinforce, I always had him read each word a minimum of five times, trying to keep his active participation by varying the stimulation technique and creating a challenge.

Sight Word Challenges

You can easily put *challenge* into repetitive reinforcement, such as "Waking Up and Putting to Sleep" and "Read and Step" as described above. Variations of activities and games can put challenge into repetitive reinforcement, I'm sure you can think of many. Here are some others to get you started.

1. *Mine or Yours?*: Take a stack of sight words, up to twenty. The challenge is for the student to get a bigger pile than you, by reading the words quickly. Words that are slow go to you. Words that are fast go to the student(s). This is a quick way to practice the medium or fastest groups of sight words. (Don't do this with the slowest pile, unless you are cruel.) When done, each person counts the cards in his or her pile, does symbol imagery exercises if necessary, and starts the challenge again with the slower cards. Thus, he or she reads the slow words again, and perhaps again.

2. *Memory*: This is good reinforcement for particularly slow or difficult words. Make two cards for each sight word, then turn the cards are turned over (asleep). Then the student and you take turns turning two words over, reading, and trying to match them to each other. When matched, the pair of words go to the "matcher." When I play the game, I often add a miscalling element to it, by miscalling one of the words I've turned over. If the student can correct me, the word has to be immediately turned back over and I lose my turn. This gives the student hold and compare stimulation and practice reading the word, while also keeping him or her attending during your turn. Students can work with each other on this challenge; small groups can take turns. Whole classes can use words that need to be taught for a specific unit or a specific lesson.

3. *Tic-Tac-Toe and Read*: Played like regular Tic-Tac-Toe, *Tic-Tac-Toe and Read* has nine sight word cards placed in front of the student in three

rows of three. You and the student take turns choosing a word to read, placing a marker on it if read accurately and *quickly*. The goal is to win Tic-Tac-Toe by accurately reading three in a row. But, the marker can't be placed on slow words, words read inaccurately, or even words that are self-corrected. The marker can only go on the word when the word is read instantly.

4. *I'm a Card*: This challenge is especially fun for small groups or whole classrooms of primary children, where many of the irregular words have to be memorized. Start with three to five sight words, printed in large lower case letters on large cards. Pass out the cards to chosen students, who then come to the front of the room and hold the cards in front of them. The teacher touches the head of one of the "cards" and chooses a student in the group or class to read the word. If read quickly and accurately, the "card" can take a step to a designated "win" spot in the room.

A variation of this is that each student in the group or class gets a card on his or her desk. The teacher identifies a student to stand and show their card. The card can be read in unison or by a specific student—and put to "sleep" on the desk if read quickly. It is fun for the class to see how many card are sleeping, and how many are still awake...yawning.

Practice and Pacing

Sight word practice must be repetitive and daily. The student must read the words many times during a given stimulation. Categorizing sight words into piles of slow, medium, and fast helps the student see progress, and allows more and more sight words to be learned, building the Visual Circle.

Begin the overlap into a sight word list, at whatever level the student is able to do symbol imagery. For example, if Buzz is able to do symbol imagery fairly well at the CVC level, then I can begin him on CVC sight words. For a beginning reader, it is helpful to begin sight words with primarily phonetically consistent words to reduce his or her frustration. However, as soon as he or she demonstrates consistency in the symbol imagery exercises, the student should be given phonetically inconsistent words. The key is to determine whether or not his symbol imagery is developed enough to help him memorize the word.

Summary

The Visual Circle is a critical, integral part of the reading process, and stands alone as an entity that must be stimulated and established for fluent reading and comprehension. Sight word development must be taken seriously, and not just thrown in as something to work on at home after dinner or on the way to school. Just as it is time well spent to develop the Auditory Circle with phonics programs, it is time well spent to develop the Visual Circle with symbol imagery exercises and repetitive reinforcement. I often explain to students that, as in sports, your body needs lots of practice to learn to shoot a basket or dribble a ball, use a skateboard or ride a bike; in learning, your brain needs lots of practice picturing words, hearing sounds, reading and spelling.

In developing sight words, it is important to remember that the goal is for immediate recognition, instant decoding, not slow phonetic processing or self-correction. Don't confuse the circles. Reading is just oral language written down. We should be able to read at the same speed we are able to talk.

Summary:
Step 7

Imaging Sight Words

> **Goal:** To build an extensive base of sight words, recognized instantly.

1. Capture and Categorize
   - Use a most commonly read list, such as the Fry list.
   - Capture the words not recognized immediately.
   - Put slow words on cards in lower case, bold letters.
   - Categorize the words into slow, medium, and fast piles.

2. Symbol image
   - Do symbol imagery exercises with sight words to place in visual memory.

3. Reinforce
   - Reinforce repetitively, moving words from slow to fast piles.
   - Use challenges to keep active attention and fun in reinforcement:
     — Wake Up and Put to Sleep
     — Read and Step
     — Tic Tac Toe and Read
     — Memory
     — Mine or Yours?
     — I'm a Card

Group Instruction

Establishing an extensive sight word base for each student is important, requiring capturing and categorizing his or her *own* sight words. Once this is completed, the same repetitive reinforcement applies. If there are five or six students such as Buzz in your class, this is an important area to give individualized attention. What else is going to make a significant difference in their lives? Not studying content, so replace a content activity with building the Visual Circle. If you can't, contact a local high school and bring in a work experience student to work daily with your students. Work experience students are free, must show up regularly, and this work may direct them toward a life of teaching.

When working with groups of students, capturing and categorizing may need to be with the collective group, with one box of sight words for the group. Repetitive reinforcement then requires you to be very observant regarding which words are difficult for which student, offering more stimulation to that student for given words. This is probably more difficult than setting up for individualized instruction!

Though specific words for specific students can't be reinforced, all the game-like challenges can be done with groups or classrooms of students. This is especially true for words in units, specific sight words you know need work, vocabulary words, terms from content, and spelling words. Words can be put on cards or on transparencies for the overhead projector—and become friends rather enemies.

16   Imaging Spelling

Sometimes it seems as if spelling is shrouded in mystery. Why do some children learn to spell so easily yet others are bewildered by it? Why are some adults good spellers and others, though very bright, unable to even use the dictionary? Why was my son, Rhett, able to spell nearly anything by age seven, yet his grandfather struggled all his life with spelling, though both had IQ's above 140? Why is spelling a friend to some, easily learned, but to others an enemy not to be trusted? Why was my mother able to spell anything at any time, in any place, barely missing a breath?

You know the answer to those questions by now. Spelling is not a mystery. As discussed earlier, it requires two primary sensory-cognitive functions that can be taught: phonemic awareness and symbol imagery—two primary *parts*, an ear and an eye, Auditory and Visual.

Phonetic processing is the fail-safe system for spelling; however, it is not how efficient spellers spell words. Efficient spellers spell from visual memory, the symbol imagery of the word. Though a few rules can be helpful, to be fast, we spell from a stored visual pattern. When we need to *verify* a word because the visual pattern is momentarily lost, we use our phonetic processing system including checking our articulatory feedback, or we use a rule, or both. The same applies when we are learning to spell a new word, which does not have an established visual pattern. We again use our phonetic processing system (our phonemic awareness to put the sounds in the right place), perhaps integrate that with a rule or two we may know or remember, look at the word to see if it matches what we remember reading, store the visual pattern in our symbol imagery, and away we go. When our underlying systems are in place, spelling is our friend, or at least, not something we have to worry about in our myriad of worries.

However, without *both* underlying systems (phonetic processing and symbol imagery), spelling becomes a puzzle. If Buzz only has the ability to sound words out when he spells, then he may spell *answer* as "anser," *explain* as "explane," …or *faucet* as "fosset." If he only has the ability to visually remember words, then his spelling will be remarkably accurate for some words (the words he has in memory) but remarkably inaccurate for others. He may spell *answer* as "anwer," or *explain* as "explian," or *faucet* as "faccuet."

This *Seeing Stars* step demonstrates how to use symbol imagery exercises for placing spelling in the visual memory system. However, along with the specific exercises, the overall development of basic symbol imagery provides students with a strengthened visual memory system from which to *unconsciously* place spelling in memory. Individuals with the cognitive tools of phonetic processing and symbol imagery don't have to study each word in English to learn to spell it; instead, they place words in memory just from exposure to print.

Providing those tools for students often requires conscious application of the previous steps of *Seeing Stars*. The technique demonstrated here, and used at all Lindamood-Bell Centers, is called "Analyze, Visualize, and Write" (AVW). Interestingly enough, I created AVW because of Jan, the college girl referred to in Chapter Seven. Back then, symbol imagery wasn't yet a part of stimulation at Lindamood-Bell, so the treatment emphasis with Jan had been nearly exclusively on phonetic processing; and, it improved her word attack ability and phonetic spelling, though both could still be quite laborious. Jan had been forced, due to academic probation, to be enrolled in a remedial reading and writing class at her community college. Because she was a hard worker and her literacy skills had improved so significantly, I hadn't worried about her grades in the class. One day, I casually asked how she was doing. She sheepishly said, with the usual grin on her face, "Not so good. I keep flunking the spelling tests."

Flabbergasted, I said, "Why? Are you studying?"

"Yes, I study really hard for each test!! It doesn't seem to help."

Though even more surprised, I thought to ask, "How are you studying?"

"I write each word ten times, sometimes twenty times, I write them over and over, but when I take the test I forget most of them."

She showed me some of her tests, and the words were phonetically accurate, but misspelled. I thought about how I spelled words, realizing again that I remembered the image of words, the look of them, especially noting certain parts to be sure to spell accurately…like ans*w*er and s*w*ord.

Jan looked like she was going to cry, partly because she thought she was letting us down and partly because she was worried and scared. I said, "Let me show you a way to study those words."

I began. "The first thing you need to know is that spelling is auditory and visual." I drew an ear and an eye. "Many parts of words you can use your ear for, just as you did on your tests, but your ear can't hear the sounds for some parts of words, and…"

"I know. I try to spell with the sounds I hear, but then I get the words wrong—not as bad as I used to, but they're still wrong!," her eyes were very intent. She was frustrated and thought it was her fault for not trying harder.

Continuing, I said, "Spelling needs both parts working, your ear and your eye. When your eye begins to work, it takes pictures of the words, then you can spell most words instantly, without having to sound them out. And, it can also help you remember parts of words that your ear can't help with. For example, read this word for me: *answer*." I wrote the word, *answer*.

Sort of laughing, "*Answer*."

"Right. Is there any part of that word that needs your eye? Is there any part that you can't use your ear?"

Looking carefully at the word and saying it over and over, using her articulatory/auditory feedback we had developed with the ADD Program, Jan said, "Oh, I can't hear the **W**."

"Right. Is that the only part of the word or is there more?"

Studying it again. "No, that's the only part. Right?"

"Right. There's one little letter in there. When you're studying spelling you'll need to *analyze* the words to know which parts don't play fair, parts that you can only know with your eye. Let's see. The next thing you'll do is cover the word, and write it in the air, so you can picture it. That's *visualizing* it."

Jan covered the word *answer*, giggling, and wrote it in the air. I had to help her say and write the letters in lower case, not jumbled on top of one another, because this was both new and difficult for her.

I continued. "As you write it, say it with the **W** sound in it—ans**w**er—just to be sure you get the irregular part in your spelling. After you do the *analyzing* and *visualizing* part, *write* in on paper.

Jan proceeded to air-write the word *answer*, saying the part that didn't play fair, and then wrote it on the paper in front of her. She analyzed, visualized and wrote. Then we did the same procedure with her other words. She left with a sheet of paper with the letters **AVW** at the top of the page, and some handwritten columns, later to become known as the *Visual Spelling Chart*.

Jan used the AVW technique tirelessly and began getting 100's on her spelling tests, passing her remedial class, eventually getting off of academic probation. Ultimately, she finished her four year degree with a B average, and has since completed a Masters Degree. I saw her a few years ago; she was unrecognizable from the vulnerable, frustrated, sensitive college girl sitting across from me unable to visualize either concepts or words.

As with the other steps of *Seeing Stars*, this step should be initiated as soon as possible, while continuing basic symbol imagery development. With that in mind, I overlap Buzz to his school spelling; however, he is still working on CCVCC basic symbol imagery and his sight words.

SAMPLE LESSON

"Symbol Imaging" Spelling Words
The Set

"Let's use the imaging part of your brain to help you study spelling words."

Nanci: *"Let's use the imaging part of your brain to help you study spelling words. Spelling is probably already getting easier for you because your brain can image now, but there are some specific things we can do to make words really stick in your mind."*

Buzz: "Great. I've always hated spelling. But, now it has been getting easier and easier, just like memorizing my sight words is getting pretty easy."

Nanci: *"That's because when you visualize those sight words to help you with reading, you are also helping yourself visualize them for spelling. Two for one!"*

Buzz: "Hmmm. I hadn't thought of that. But, when I have to write sentences now, some of my sight words are the same words I use in the sentences—and I can spell them. You're right."

Nanci: *"Naturally…"*

Lesson

Nanci: *"Let's start. Here is your spelling word, **before**. First I want you to analyze it to see which part you have to remember."*

> "First I want you to analyze it to see which part you have to remember."

Buzz: "I have to remember all of it!"

Nanci: *"That's for sure, but what part doesn't play fair? There is one letter in there you might forget when you go to remember the word!"*

Buzz: "Hmmm. Let me see. (A small hand touching each letter and saying the sounds.) The **e**?"

Nanci: *"Right. You might forget to put that **e** in there. So, underline the letter **e** and then cover the word and write it in the air…say the letters as you write, just like we usually do."*

> "You might forget to put that **e** in there. So, underline the letter **e** and then cover the word and write it in the air…say the letters as you write, just like we usually do."

Buzz: "That's easy. (Marks a line under the letter **e**—befor<u>e</u>—covers the word with his left hand, and air-writes with his right. He is right-handed.) **B–E–F–O–R–E**."

Nanci: *"Perfect. Now keep the word covered up, and write it on paper so you can check to see if you're right."*

> "Now keep the word covered, and write it on paper so you can check if you're right."

Buzz: "I'm right! I can still visualize it." (Does it anyway, writing *before* on the paper.)

Nanci: *"Great. Now uncover the first one and see for sure that you are correct."*

"Now uncover the first one and see for sure that you are correct."

Buzz: "See. I told you I could still visualize it. I'm right. (Uncovering *before*, comparing his response to stimulus word.)

Nanci: *"You certainly are right. That's a good way to study your spelling words. We call it Analyze, Visualize, and Write—AVW. And, here is the same thing only on a chart I made for you. We'll use it to keep track of the spelling words you are working on, just like we are keeping track of your sight words."*

Buzz and I proceed to use the *Visual Spelling Chart* (see below) for the spelling words he couldn't spell instantly.

Lesson Summary:
"Symbol Imaging" Spelling Words

- Student *analyzes* the word for phonetic inconsistency.
- Student marks the phonetic inconsistency, lightly so as not to disturb the visual pattern of the word.
- Student *visualizes* the word, air-writing and saying letters.
- Student *writes* the word on paper.
- Student compares response to stimulus—uncovering stimulus and comparing with written response.

Application of AVW to the Visual Spelling Chart (VSC) is very easy for students; the chart being a means of capturing and cataloguing spelling words—similar to capturing and categorizing sight words. Words that can't be spelled instantly are written on the chart *by the teacher* to be sure the print is perfect, ensuring accurate imagery. The words can be captured from spelling lists, the 1000 most common words, spelling errors from paragraph writing, or content specific terminology.

The four columns on the VSC represent the following:

- ANALYZE: Analyzing irregularity and lightly marking the word
- VISUALIZE: Emphasizing irregularity and air-writing word, saying each letter
- WRITE: Writing word on paper and saying the whole word as writing
- TRACK: Noting spelling accuracy to know when a word is in long term memory

Here is an example of VSC in use.

Visual Spelling Chart

Follow the steps for each column.

Analyze Mark: ·Syllables ·Accent ·Unfair	Visualize · Print word with visual cue. - Say word as it looks · See/write in air	Write · Say while write	· Date and chec Date:			
1. have	have	have				
2. an\swer	answer	answer				
3. pre\si\dent	president	president				
4.						

Practice and Pacing

The *Seeing Stars* program has prepared students for this moment of using imagery for spelling. Unlike Jan, your students will know what it means to visualize and write the letters in the air! We had the cart before the horse with Jan, but then we didn't know what the horse was and thus didn't know how to develop it first. You have created the horse by doing all the previous steps of symbol imagery, making this last step easy, though necessary nonetheless.

Practicing spelling with imagery can be accomplished with or without the VSC. But, the chart helps catalogue and track words needing more reinforcement. Often, the VSC accumulates numerous words to be put in memory, though they soon leave the chart. A long list of working words is to be expected because of the *gap* remedial students may have prior to learning symbol imagery. For example, Buzz came to us spelling at a high-first grade level, but he was in fifth grade. Consequently, his was a four-year-large gap, and closing it meant many words on the chart. But, as he became a better reader, and saw words in print, his now developed visual memory system began to automatically store words in his spelling lexicon. In other words, reading and spelling began to work together, one supporting the other.

Summary

Writing is oral language on paper to convey meaning; spelling is a *part* of writing and a partner to reading. They walk hand in hand down the road of literacy. Perhaps the mystery of spelling is that there has ever been any mystery at all. It is a simple process of integration in the sensory system: phonemic awareness with symbol imagery.

Good *writing* is puzzling, however. What enables someone to have good sentence structure, a high vocabulary, creative story plots, interesting characters, humor, passion, in their writing? What makes a Hemingway or a Tolstoy? That may be a mystery, but not spelling *words*.

Summary:
Step 8

Imaging, Reading & Spelling Two Syllables

> **Goal:** To develop symbol imagery for an instant base of spelling words, automatically extended during the act of reading.

1. Capture and Catalogue
- Use most common spelling word list, such as Fry.
- Capture the words not spelled instantly.
- Put slow words on Visual Spelling Chart in lower case letters.
- Catalogue the words on the chart to know which are able to be spelled instantly and which need more stimulation.

2. Analyze, Visualize, and Write on the Visual Spelling Chart
- Student analyzes the word for phonetic irregularity.
- Student marks the phonetic inconsistency, lightly so as not to disturb the visual pattern of the word.
- Student visualizes the word, air-writing and saying letters.
- Student writes the word on paper.
- Student compares response to stimulus—uncovering stimulus and comparing with written response.

Group Instruction

Establishing an extensive spelling word base for each student is important, requiring capturing and cataloguing his or her spelling words on the Visual Spelling Chart (VSC). Once this is completed, the same repetitive reinforcement applies. Since this requires some individualized attention, this is another area requiring use of a class assistant such as a work experience student, parent volunteer, or even peer tutoring by a good speller in the class.

When working with groups of students, capturing and categorizing may need to be with the collective group, with one VSC for the group, though each student can keep a separate record of their difficult words. However, the technique of AVW is easily used with large or small groups, and is particularly fun with an overhead projector or chalkboard. The analysis part of the task can be done by specific students you have called on, thumbs up or down with others. Covering the analyzed word on the overhead or chalkboard, the visualizing and writing part of the activity can be with the whole group or class, each writing in the air at their desks and then writing on paper. Uncovering the word, each student can compare their writing to the stimulus word. My experience with classroom use of the AVW technique has been that words usually forgotten by the worst spellers, are magically and mysteriously remembered at the weekly spelling test.

17

Imaging, Reading & Spelling Two Syllables

It was raining outside. Buzz came in, stomped the water and mud off his shoes, went over and sat down. He had a library book in his hands. With his head slightly down, he looked sad and frustrated. Hearing me come over, he looked up and said, "I'm better in reading now, especially the little words, but long words are still pretty hard." I sat down next to him.

Intact single syllable processing doesn't guarantee intact multisyllable processing. Consequently, reading and spelling multisyllable words often exposes weakness in basic sensory-cognitive functions. *Immigration* becomes "imagination" in reading, *necessary* becomes "nessissary" in spelling, despite good single syllable phonemic awareness and symbol imagery skills. Though multisyllables are single syllables put together, direct instruction and stimulation is needed to ensure decoding and encoding accuracy and self-correction.

Often outside the memorized word base, multisyllable words are the majority of what children and adults may have to process phonetically. Unfamiliar long words, names, technical terms, etc., often have to be "sounded-out." And, multisyllable words begin in first grade. Since their processing can't be assumed and they are very important to the literacy game, they deserve your undivided attention at this late juncture in my book. Tired though you may be, gear up for this last section. I'll present it to you in parts, each part experienced through our Buzz.

Seeing Stars shoots into multisyllables by teaching suffixes as imaged chunks, then sequencing sounds and letters at the multisyllable level, concluding with applying the imagery to reading and spelling multisyllable words. The three basic aspects of multisyllable stimulation are as follows.

• IMAGING AFFIXES:	Imagery for prefixes and suffixes, stored and retrieved as chunks for instant reading and spelling.

- IMAGING & SEQUENCING: Imagery for sequencing sounds and letters within syllables, using the *Multisyllable Board*.

- READING & SPELLING: Imagery application to processing nonsense words and memorizing an extended sight word base.

Imaging Affixes

The imagery stimulation begins with the *parts* of the multisyllable words, building toward the *whole* of decoding/encoding. The parts are often the affixes—suffixes and prefixes—that provide a morphological structure for English. Though numerous, affixes are easily imaged and placed in memory. We'll begin "imaging affixes" with the most frequently used suffixes: ple (maple), tle (little), dle (paddle), kle (sparkle), ble (bubble), fle (rifle), gle (gargle), zle (puzzle), cle (circle), sle (hassle). Next we'll do suffixes such as: ly (lovely), tion (nation), ture (nature), ous (famous), ment (department), tive (active), and cious (gracious), etc. (See the Appendix for common suffixes and prefixes.)

Suffixes are taught as visual units, to be imaged and stored for instant reading and spelling recognition. Here is Buzz, "symbol imaging" common suffixes, some of which aren't phonetically consistent.

SAMPLE LESSON

Imaging Suffixes for Instant Decoding and Encoding

Counting syllables:

"How many chunks or syllables in my name, Nanci."

The Set

Nanci: *"You've gotten pretty good at imaging one syllable words, words that have one beat. You learned to count syllables in school, right?"*

Buzz: "Yes. My teacher taught us to count by clapping our hands."

Nanci: *"Great. Let's do that. How many chunks or syllables in my name, Nanci."*

Buzz: "Two." (He said my name and clapped his hands twice.)

Nanci: *"Instead of just clapping, let's put two colored squares down for those beats."*

Buzz: "OK." (He placed two colored squares on the table in front of him.)

We checked his first name and his last name, then a few other words ranging from one to five syllables. Each time he placed colored squares to designate the syllable. He didn't have to say the syllables accurately or note sounds; he just had to represent the number of syllables just as he would with clapping. Any representation would do, even 3X5 cards. This was a relatively easy task for him because it only required a gross judgment of auditory processing.

Nanci: *"Now, we're going to visualize endings of words, called suffixes. They are parts of words that come at the end and pretty much look the same every time."*

Lesson

Nanci: *"A word like lovely has one of those endings. Let's visualize it. First tell me how many chunks does lovely have?"*

Teaching the suffix: ly

Buzz: "*Lovely*. Two." (Placing two colored squares.)

Nanci: *"Here's two lines on this paper, one for each chunk, say and write the word lovely on it."* (I drew two lines: _____ _____.)

Buzz: "*Lovely*. (He wrote *love* on one line, but stopped at the second line.) Lee. I don't know how to write that. Is it an **L** and an **E**, or two **EE**'s, or a **Y**? I don't know for sure."

Suffixes are imaged and then written in the air	Nanci: *"Let me show you the word—and you find the ending and image it."* (I write the word **lovely** on a piece of paper.)
	Buzz: *"Lovely. Oh, its **LY**."*
	Nanci: *"Right. **LY** says lee, because the letter **Y** often says /ee/ at the end of words. Now, finish writing the word on your paper. And, I'll show you **LY** on a card to visualize.* (Buzz completed writing love-ly on the paper.)
"Now touch and say each chunk, then cover the word—and see and say it."	*"Now touch and say each chunk, then cover the word—and see and say it. Writing it in the air, please."*
	Buzz: *"Lovely. **L–O–V–E–L–Y**."*
	Nanci: *"Great. What's the last chunk you saw?"*
	Buzz: *"**L–Y**."* (Saying and air-writing the word again, before answering.)
"What's the last chunk you saw?"	Nanci: *"Exactly. And here it is on a card. (I hold up the suffix card with **ly**.) Got it? (Taking it away.) What does it say and what letters did you see?"*
	Buzz: *"Lee, **L–Y**."*
	Nanci: *"Now you understand a little about these suffixes that come at the end of words. This time I'm going to show you some cards with endings on them and I'll tell you what they say. Then we'll do imaging exercises."*
	Buzz: *"OK."*
	Teaching the suffixes: **ple, tle, etc.**
Teaching the le's:	Nanci: *"Here is the card **P-L-E** and it says **pl** at the end of words. The **e** doesn't say any sound at all, its just there to make a syllable, a chunk, because every chunk has to have a vowel letter. See it, say it, and write it in the air...please."* (I take the **ple** card away.)

Buzz: "*Pl*, **P–L–E**." (Saying and writing in air.)

Nanci: *"Great Here's another one with the **E** at the end (holding up the **tle** card), and it says tl. See, say, and write…please!"*

Buzz: "Easy, *tl*, **T–L–E**."

Teaching the suffix: **tion**

Teaching tion:

We continued with all the **le** endings, and then went for one more suffix, an irregular one, but very, very common.

Nanci: *"The last one we'll learn today will be this. (I show him the **tion** card.) And, it doesn't sound like it looks! It says shun."*

Nanci holds up "tion" card, then takes it away.

Buzz: "Weird. There isn't /sh/!" (We would have analyzed the irregularity, if he hadn't noticed it.)

Nanci: *"Really weird, you're right. But, one thing is great about this ending—it always says shun. No*

Break the word with a light diagonal line.	*trickery. So once you visualize it, you have it for good. See, say, and write it…let's get it in your head!" (I hold up the ending card **tion**, then take it away.)*
	Buzz: "**T-I-O-N**, *shun.* I know I've seen it before."
"What's the last chunk you see?"	Nanci: *"I'm sure you have. It's in a lot of words, like **nation**, **lotion**, **motion**. (I write the words on a piece of paper.) Take your pencil and mark off the syllable with a diagonal line, not a straight line. Like this. (I show him **na/tion**.)*
	*"The reason I want you to use a diagonal line is that your imagery for the word won't get disturbed with a diagonal, but a straight line might make you think the letter **L** is in the word."*
"Altogether, chunk by chunk."	Buzz: "Like this?" (He marks the words: **lo/tion, mo/tion**.)
	Nanci: *"Right. Now, cover them and see, say, and write the word lotion for me. But, do it chunk by chunk. Lo-tion."*
	Buzz: "Hmmm. *Lo,* **L-O**—*shun,* **T-I-O-N**."
	Nanci: *"Great. What's the last chunk you see?"*
Reinforce suffixes for instant reading and spelling	Buzz: "*Shun,* **T-I-O-N**."
	Nanci: *"Great again. What's the first chunk you see?"*
	Buzz: " *Lo,* **L-O**."

Lesson Summary:
Imaging Suffixes for Instant Decoding and Encoding

- Student(s) counts syllables (chunks), designating them with colored squares.

- Teacher presents the concept that words have endings (suffixes) and every ending has a vowel letter.

- Student(s) images the suffix from the suffix card.

- Student(s) sees, says, and air-writes each suffix.

- Do symbol imagery exercises for the whole word, chunk by chunk.

- Practice reading and spelling suffixes until recognized instantly.

- Present common suffixes first: ly, le's, tion—adding suffixes as appropriate.

After Buzz has learned a few common suffixes, he is overlapped to *Imaging Syllables*. As he is sequencing sounds and letters in syllables, more suffixes can be added to his repertoire (See the Appendix). For example, he could be taken into the suffix grid of the ADD program, a systematic approach to teaching irregular suffixes. However suffixes are presented, he must learn them as imaged chunks, and read and spell them *instantly*.

Sequencing Letters on the Multisyllable Board

If reading and spelling multisyllable words was as easy as imaging suffixes, Buzz would be flying by now. But, it is not—and he is not. *Reading and spelling multisyllable words requires the ability to perceive and image sounds and letters within each chunk.*

The following sample lesson demonstrates Buzz learning to apply his single syllable symbol imagery and instant recognition of suffixes to sequencing letters in two syllable words. As in single syllable processing, the words are nonsense and presented in a chain. He uses the Multisyllable Board, allowing him to image letters on visual chunks. The Multisyllable Board is a continuation of the Syllable Board, only the board now illustrates syllables, three parts to be imaged—a prefix, a core, and a suffix (the parts are designated by three different colors). This concretizes the task prior to imaging in the air and writing on paper. If you don't have a multisyllable board, one can easily be created with a nine inch piece of poster board, two inches high, broken into three equal parts.

S A M P L E   L E S S O N

Multisyllable Board:
Sequencing Letters in Two Syllables

The Set

Nanci: *"You're ready to start applying your endings to a new task. Remember when we used the Syllable Board for imaging and writing letters?"*

Buzz: "Yeah…" (Smiling…and squinting.)

Nanci: *"Well, now we're going to do the same thing, only its a longer board that holds three chunks. We'll start with two chunks, a core and one of your endings."*

Buzz: "What is a core?"

"Here's the Multisyllable Board. This middle square is the core part, and the other colored squares are for the beginnings and endings."

Nanci: *"The core chunk is like an apple core—a middle part. Your words will have a core. And, the core will have imaginary letters on it, just like the syllable board did. Easy huh? Just a core and an ending.*

Buzz: "Sounds OK… so far."

	Nanci: *"Here's the Multisyllable Board. This middle square is the core part, and the other colored squares are for the beginnings and endings."* (I showed Buzz the multisyllable board.)
	Buzz: "Hmmm. OK. Here's the core part and the ending part. (Touching the middle and last squares.) What's this first part for?" (Referring to the left side of the board, where a prefix will go.)
"Only one sound will change at a time on the core, but maybe a whole ending will change."	Nanci: *"That's where you will image beginnings, prefixes, and then we will have three syllables. The word will grow from two to three syllables.*
	Buzz: "Hmmm…"
	Nanci: *"Here's the last thing for you to know about doing this. Only one sound will change at a time on the core, but maybe a whole ending will change."*
"Now, start here (pointing to the core) and say and touch each chunk — then image and write the letters on the board."	Buzz: "Mm."

Lesson

	Nanci: *"Let's begin. How many chunks do you hear when I say the word iply?"*
	Buzz: *"Iply.* Two."
	Nanci: *"Great. Now, start here (pointing to the core) and say and touch each chunk—then image and write the letters on the board."*
	Buzz: *"Iply. Ip-ly.* **I-P…L-Y**. (He says each chunk, writing imaginary letters on both chunks.)
"What is the last chunk you visualize?"	Nanci: *"What is the last chunk you visualize?"*
	Buzz: "Ly, **L-Y**. That's my **L-Y** ending."
	Nanci: *"Right. And, if you couldn't visualize it, I would get out the **ly** card so you could see it, and maybe even put it on the ending chunk for awhile. But, since my goal is for you to be able to image these*

171

chunks, I don't want to have an ending card out there very long. Then you could just see it, rather than image it!"

Buzz: "I can picture it in my mind. Really."

Nanci: *"I know. And, that's what you need to do when you spell and read. Let's say, see, and write each of the chunks again. Iply. Then we'll change it."*

Buzz: "Iply. Ip-ly. **I-P...L-Y.**"

Nanci: *"Great. Change iply to aply. Say and touch the old and the new word on the multisyllable board."*

Buzz: "Like this? *Iply to aply.* (Saying and touching each chunk as he said the old and new words.)

Nanci: *"Perfect. Which chunk changed."*

Buzz: "Hmmm. *Iply...aply.* The first one changed. *Ip* to *ap.*"

Nanci: *"Excellent. Now say and write ap on the first chunk and ly on the last chunk."*

Buzz: *"Ap-ly.* **A-P...L-Y.** (Saying and writing the letters.)

Nanci: *"You said the two chunks that were changing, and that was great. That's exactly what I want you to do for awhile—say the chunk to the chunk. Ip to ap, or whatever the old and new words are. Get it?"*

Buzz: "I think so. It's kind of easy if I visualize the old and new ones. At least it seems easy."

Nanci: *"It is easy when you are visualizing the words, but when you're not, it can be pretty hard. That's why we walked up a ladder in teaching your brain to image the letters. We started with one letter, then more and more letters as we made words, and*

"Change *iply* to *aply.* Say and touch the old and the new word on the multisyllable board."

"...say the chunk to the chunk. *Ip* to *ap...*"

172

"Change *aply* to *aption*. Remember to say the old and new word, and the chunk to the chunk."

"Say the word again, and write the letters, chunk by chunk. *Aption*."

"Now say and write the letters for the whole word, including the ending. Remember, do it chunk by chunk."

"What's the third letter you see in the first chunk?"

---

now you're visualizing little parts of words to make long words. Good on you! Good on your brain."

Buzz: "Hmmm. So far, this isn't too hard. Give me some more."

Nanci: *"OK. Change aply to aption. Remember to say the old and new word, and the chunk to the chunk."*

Buzz: *"Aply…aption.* (Saying and touching the board.) Hmmm. The ending changed. *Aply* to *aption*. *Ly* changes to *tion*, **T-I-O-N**. (Saying and writing the imaginary letters on the board.)

Nanci: *"Excellent. Excellent. And, you said the chunk to the chunk!"*

Buzz: "This is pretty easy…so far."

Nanci: *"OK. Say the word again, and write the letters, chunk by chunk. Aption."*

Buzz: *"Ap-tion.* **A-P…T-I-O-N**."

Nanci: *"Great. I always want you to visualize the chunks not the whole word all together. As we get into more letters and more syllables, visualizing the whole word all at once is too hard, but visualizing the word chunk by chunk is easy."*

Buzz: "OK."

Nanci: *"Change aption to faption."*

Buzz: *"Aption* to *faption* (saying and touching the board for each chunk). *Ap* changes to *fap*."

Nanci: *"Great. Now say and write the letters for the first chunk."*

Buzz: *"Fap.* **F-A-P**."

Nanci: *"Super. Now say and write the letters for the whole word, including the ending. Remember, do it chunk by chunk."*

Buzz: *"Faption.* **F-A-P...T-I-O-N***."*

Nanci: *"What's the third letter you see in the first chunk?"*

Buzz: "Hmmm. The first chunk? *Faption.* (He says *fap*, and touches each imaginary letter, but doesn't rewrite each one.) **P**!"

Nanci: *"Great. That's right. What's the second letter you see?"*

Buzz: "Easy. The **A**."

Nanci: *"Can you still see the ending?"*

Buzz: "Easy. **T-I-O-N**, *tion.*"

Nanci: *"I'll give you a few more. Change faption to fantion."*

Buzz: "*Faption* to *fantion. Fap* to *fan,* the **P** changes to an **N**."

Nanci: *"Great. And, say and write the whole word on the board—chunk by chunk."*

Buzz: "Easy. *Fantion.* **F-A-N...T-I-O-N**." (Saying and writing on the board.)

Nanci: *"What's that first chunk?"*

Buzz: "*Fan.* **F-A-N**."

Nanci: *"You're definitely getting this. Let's do another one. Change fantion to frantion."*

Buzz: "*Fan* changes to *fran.* Add an **R**. **F-R-A-N**. (Saying and writing the letters on the board.)"

Nanci: *"Excellent. Now, say, image, and write the whole word, chunk by chunk."*

Buzz: "*Frantion.* **F-R-A-N...T-I-O-N**." (Saying and writing letters on the board.)

"*...say and write the whole word on the board — chunk by chunk.*"

"*What's the fourth letter you see in the first chunk?*"

174

Have the student image spelling patterns

Nanci: *"What's the fourth letter you see in the first chunk?"*

Buzz: *"Frantion. Fran.* **N.***"*

Nanci: *"Yup. See you can do this easily. It's just like those one syllable words we did—and you were really good at that before we started this. Here's the last one. Change frantion to fraction."*

Buzz: *"Frantion to fraction. Fran to frac.* **F-R-A-K.** Wait. Isn't that a real word?"

Nanci: *"Yup. And, you got all the sounds in the right place, but there are two letters that make the /k/ sound. The* **K** *and..."*

Buzz: "The **C.** **F-R-A-C.**"

Nanci: *"Right. Most of the time when you hear the /k/ sound it will be written with the letter* **C.** *So, say and write the whole word on the board, chunk by chunk."*

"Most of the time when you hear the /k/ sound it will be written with the letter C. So, say and write the whole word on the board, chunk by chunk."

Buzz: "Fraction. **F-R-A-C...T-I-O-N.** (Saying and writing the imaginary letters on the board.)

Nanci: *"What's the last letter in the first chunk?"*

Buzz: "The **C!** **F-R-A-C.** Hmmm. I spelled a pretty long word, didn't I? When are we going to use this other part?"

Nanci: *"We'll use that when we learn beginnings, prefixes. Pretty soon."*

175

> ## Lesson Summary:
> ### *Multisyllable Board: Sequencing Letters at Two Syllables*
>
> - Teacher says two syllable words, in a chain.
> - Either a letter changes in the core syllable or a suffix changes, but not both.
> - Use chains that focus on changing the letter just prior to the suffix.
> - Student(s) says, images, and air-writes each chunk on the Multisyllable Board.
> - Do symbol imagery exercises for each chunk.
> - Do symbol imagery exercises for the whole word, chunk by chunk.
> - Be sure symbol imagery is consistent with English spelling rules.

As the days and lessons continued with Buzz, we practiced more chains of two syllable words, and he visualized more suffixes. It is important to note that his retention of the suffixes was good because his basic symbol imagery was good. In the years past, when he had been exposed to affixes, he couldn't remember them, one of the complaints of his third grade teacher and certainly one of his frustrations. Now, however, his cognitive tool box was filling with cognitive processes, and he was easily able to do what many other children around him had done for years. Why he hadn't been able to do what they did so easily had been a source of great puzzlement to him, a mystery; his conclusion was that he was just not as smart as the others, a little slower, perhaps dumb or stupid. His self-image had been damaged, his wings wounded. They were mending, however.

Application to Reading and Spelling Two Syllable Words

After developing imagery for sounds and letters, students are given specific application to reading and spelling two syllable words. The goal is twofold: 1) *increase the phonetic processing speed*, the Auditory Circle, by having students decode and encode nonsense words, and 2) *increase the amount of words recognized instantly*, the Visual Circle, by imaging, storing and retrieving the most common two, three, and four syllable words. By increasing both the Auditory and

Visual Circles to a level of automaticity, students are prepared for the sensory integration necessary for contextual fluency and accuracy—the final step of *Seeing Stars*.

Now that Buzz can image and sequence sounds and letters in two syllable words, he is able to monitor and self-correct his response to the stimulus when reading and spelling. He is ready to begin reading and spelling "Long Words." The first lesson is how to break them apart.

SAMPLE LESSON

Breaking Multisyllable Words and Open/Closed Syllables

Breaking two syllables:

The Set

Nanci: *"Now that you can visualize the letters in two syllable words, using the Multisyllable Board, you can begin to read and spell two syllable words. Some words will be nonsense, so you can practice the breaking rules, and some words will be real so we can add them to your sight vocabulary cards—getting your Visual Circle bigger and bigger!"*

Buzz: "OK. When I try to read those longer words in my school books I sometimes I see my endings."

Lesson

Nanci: *"Right. Two syllable words are all over the place and a big help in reading them is to know where to break the word. Once its broken, you are really just reading two little words and then putting them together.*

Buzz: "Hmmm…"

Nanci: *"There's really only three rules you need to know about reading two syllable words:*

1) Find and break in front of an ending.

Beaking rules:

1) Find and break in front of an ending.

2) Find and break between double letters.

3) Start a syllable with a consonant, if you can.

4) Break in front of a suffix.

177

2) Find and break between double letters.

3) Start a syllable with a consonant, if you can.

"We'll go over these one at a time."

Buzz: "Hmmm. OK."

Finding and breaking in front of a suffix:

Finding and breaking in front of a suffix:

Nanci: *"Here's the first word to find and break in front of the ending. (I wrote **vaction**.) Touch the ending with your finger. Now, make a diagonal line with your pencil—very lightly so it doesn't look like the letter **L**."*

Buzz: "Like this? (First he touched the suffix *tion*, then marked the word as *vac/tion*).

Nanci: *"Perfect. Touch and say the ending, then go back and read the rest of the word with it."*

Buzz: "**T-I-O-N** says *shun*, and the first part says…*vac*. *Vaction*. (He touched the ending first, then went back and touched the first part, said it, and put the word together.)

Nanci: *"Vaction. Good job. Real word?"*

Buzz: "No! Though it sort of sounds like vacation."

"Touch and say the ending, then go back and read the rest of the word with it."

Nanci: *"Right. It's not a real word and it does sort of sound like vacation. (I'm not ready to explore the difference since it would take quite a lot of time, thus a lot of lesson energy. Most importantly, he is not yet sequencing sounds/letters in three syllable words so we could get pretty far off track…a no, no. I need to keep my focus.)*

*"Break this word." (I wrote **penture**.)*

Buzz: "My ending is the **T-U-R-E**, *chur*."

Nanci: *"Great. Read the word. Touch and say the ending first if you need to, then put the word together from front to back."*

Breaking between doubles.

Teach the open/closed syllable rule.

Buzz: *"Chur. Nap...ture, napture."* (He first identified the suffix by touching and saying it, then read the rest of the word.)

Nanci: *"Right. See, these long words are really short words put together so it's easy to read them."*

Buzz: "So far, this is pretty easy. It helps me to find the ending first."

Breaking between doubles, and teaching the open/closed syllable rule:

Nanci: *"Right. And, that's good for now, but later you'll start from the beginning of the word and just read right through it. Let's do this word. (I wrote tabble.) You can find your ending, but an easier thing to do is break between double letters, the two letters that are the same."*

Buzz: "There are two **B**'s, does my line go right between them?"

Nanci: *"Yes, a diagonal line, right between them."*

Buzz: "OK. Like this?" (He wrote tab/ble.)

Nanci: *"Perfect. Now here's something to know that will help you read the word, and it will help you read and spell a lot of other words also. Touch the first syllable, and now touch the vowel in the first syllable."*

Buzz: "OK." (He touches the vowel in the first chunk—the **a**.)

Nanci: *"Think of your diagonal line in the word as a cliff. Is your vowel OPEN next to the cliff or does it have a letter guarding it from the cliff?"*

Buzz: "I think it has the letter **B** guarding it. Right?"

In an open syllable the vowel says its name: *ta/ble.*

In a closed syllable the vowel says its sound: *tab/ble.*

Nanci: *"Exactly. If the vowel has someone guarding it, it is CLOSED and if it is right next to the cliff it is OPEN."*

Buzz: "OK. This vowel is closed in from the cliff."

Nanci: *"Right. A closed vowel can say its sound, so it would say /a/.*

Buzz: "So, the first chunk says *tab.* Right?"

Nanci: *"Exactly, again. Now, put your ending with it and you have read the word."*

Buzz: "*Tabble.*"

Nanci: *"Right again. Now, here's another word. (I wrote table.) Are there double letters?"*

Buzz: "No. But...I see an ending. Should I mark it?"

Nanci: *"Yup."*

Buzz: "Hmmm." (He marked it as *ta/ble.*)

Nanci: *"Perfect. Now, touch the first syllable and then touch the vowel in the first syllable. Is the vowel open or closed? Remember, it's open if it is right next to the cliff."*

Buzz: "No guard—it's open. It's right next to the cliff."

Nanci: *"Yup. And, here's the fun thing for you to know. If the vowel is open, with nobody next to it by the line, it can say it's name...like it's going to fall off and as it goes over it says it's name. What is the name of the vowel you are touching?"*

Buzz: "**A**. It's name is **A**. Oh, the word is *table*. A real word! I thought so, but I wasn't really sure...hmmm, now I know why it says *table*...now maybe I'll be able to spell it."

Nanci: *"Right, and now we'll use our other **le** endings and practice some more open/closed words. Words like this (I wrote out buggle and bugle, mapple and maple) you can divide by finding the doubles or the endings—then decide if the vowel is open or closed. Try this one." (I pointed to bugle.)*

We continued to practice reading and spelling with the open/closed rule until he began to grasp the concept with a fair level of automaticity. The next day we practiced again, and overlapped to the third breaking rule, while continuing to reinforce.

Start a syllable with a consonant, if you can:

Start a syllable with a consonant, if you can.

Nanci: *The last really helpful thing to know about breaking long words into short words is this: Start a syllable with a consonant, if you can. For example, in this word. (I wrote out the word **human**.) This word has two vowels, so you're pretty sure it has two syllables. But, where you break it can help you read the word."*

Buzz: "Hmmm…"

Nanci: *"You have to decide where to put your line. Like with these words." (I wrote out **hu/man** and **hum/an**.) "Which one of those words starts a syllable with a consonant rather than a vowel?"*

Buzz: "The first word starts the chunk with a consonant." (He pointed to hu/man.)

Nanci: *"Right, and that is important because it helps you read the word more easily. For example, is the vowel open or closed in that word? Touch it and tell me it's sound too." (He looks at **hu/man**.)*

Buzz: "The vowel is open, so it says it's name…**U**. Hmmm. I thought so, the word is *human*!"

Nanci: *"Right! Breaking it right helped you read it right. If you broke it wrong, you might read it wrong and say humman…then you might think the word meant you were humman a song or humman along! And, that could give you the wrong image when you're reading a story! Words create images you know."*

Buzz: "I know. The reason I used to hate to read was because I read words wrong a lot, or slowly, and then I got weird pictures in my mind that didn't make sense. I thought reading was stupid."

Nanci: *"Well. It won't have to be that way anymore. Reading and spelling are going to be your friends…and, they'll be your friends for life."*

Buzz: "I'm starting to believe you…"

The Lesson Summary:
Breaking Multisyllable Words and Open/Closed Syllables

- Present and practice three basic breaking rules:

   —Find and break in front of an ending.

   —Find and break between double letters.

   —Start a syllable with a consonant, if you can.

- Teach the open/closed syllable rule for reading and spelling.

   —The vowel says its name if *open* next to the syllable line.

   —The vowel says its sound if *closed* next to the syllable line.

Buzz practiced breaking words accurately; and we overlapped into reading and spelling two syllable words, using symbol imagery. As we do at Lindamood-Bell Centers, breaking begins with a pencil, moves to a finger, and then to the eye. We call it: pencil-break (make a light line with the pencil to designate the break), finger-break (use a finger to designate the break), and then eye-break (look at the word and *see* the breaks). After reading a few cards and suffixes, Buzz begins with pencil-breaking.

S A M P L E   L E S S O N

Reading and Imaging Two Syllable Words

Reading and Imaging Two Syllables: Changing one card at a time

Student reads and images a syllable card plus a suffix.

The Set

Nanci: *"Let's practice reading and imaging two syllables words. We'll start with some cards and put words together with a core and an ending. I'll change only one card at a time."*

Buzz: "OK."

Lesson

Nanci: *"Here is a core card, **gad,** and one of your endings, **ly**. I'll put them together for you to read. You won't have to break the word, because the cards break it for you. (I show him the two cards together: **gad ly**.) What does this say?"*

Buzz: *"Gadly."*

Nanci: *"Right. (I covered the cards.) Say and write the letters in the air for **gadly**, but do it chunk by chunk."*

Buzz: "Easy. *Gad-ly,* **G-A-D...L-Y**." (Saying and air-writing.)

Nanci: *"Now, I'll change just one card, and you read it for me. I'll take out the **gad** card and bring in the **fap** card. (Now he has the two cards, **fap ly,** in front of him.) Read it, please."*

Buzz: "Now it says *faply.*"

"Say and write the letters in the air." (Covering the cards.)

Nanci: *"Right. Say and write the letters in the air."* *(Covering the cards.)*

Buzz: "Easy. *Fap-ly,* **F-A-P...L-Y**." (Saying and air-writing.)

Nanci: *"What's the last letter in the first chunk?"*

Buzz: "**P**." (Looking up, he told me what he saw, *without* having to count each letter with his hand.)

Nanci: *Right again. What might it say if I move the **ly** card over to cover up the letter **P**? Like this."* *(Now he has the two cards in front of him with **fa ly,** and I'm wanting to be sure he processes the open/closed syllable rule.)*

"...now what would it say if I take out the ly card and bring in the tion card?"

Buzz: "*F/a/*...Oh. The letter **A** is now open, so it says its name. *Fae/ly.*"

Nanci: *"Exactly. And, now what would it say if I take out the **ly** card and bring in the **tion** card?"* *(Now he has **fap tion** in front of him.)*

Buzz: "*Faption.*"

Nanci: *"Excellent. And now?"* *(I move the **tion** card to cover the letter **P**, so now he has fation in front of him.)*

Buzz: "The letter **A** is open again. It says *fae-shun.* Like nation."

Nanci: *"Yup. (Covering the cards.) And, tell me the letters you visualize for **fation**...then do **nation**!"*

Buzz: "Arg...me and my big mouth!"

I introduce reading two syllable to Buzz with syllable cards, used in a number of programs, including the ADD Program. Though this can be good initial stimulation for reading, be sure you create words that are consistent with English spelling patterns. For example, putting the **gad** card with the **ly** card to make the nonsense word *gadly* is fine because we have words in English using that orthographic pattern (*gladly*). But, changing the **ly** ending to **tion** to make *gadtion* would not make an orthographic pattern consistent with English, and should not be done with students. We don't have the letter **D** in front of the **tion** suffix. Be careful in using this step and perhaps use it primarily to practice the open/closed rule or don't use it at all. Instead immediately have students "*break and read.*"

SAMPLE LESSON

"Breaking, Reading, and Imaging"
two syllable words from lists or cards

Nanci: *"Here is a list of two syllable nonsense words for you to read. This list practices the endings you know instantly, so it will be pretty easy for you."*

Buzz: *"OK."*

Nanci: *"I want you to break the word apart with a diagonal line…like this…(demonstrating) and, do it very lightly so it won't look like the letter **L**."*

Buzz: *"OK."*

Nanci: *"Break and read this word. (I wrote lanture.)*

Buzz: *"There's the ture ending (He broke it as: lan/ture.) Lan…ture, lanture."*

Nanci: *"Yup. Easy. Tell me the letters you see. (Covering the word.)*

Buzz: **"L-A-N…T-U-R-E**. *Lanture."*

Nanci: *"Excellent. Here's another word to break and read."* (I wrote taption.)

Student breaks, reads, and images words from lists.

Buzz: *"Tap…tion. Taption."* (Breaking as *tap/tion*, Buzz very quickly read the word.)

Nanci: *"Great. See it and say each letter. You don't have to write it in the air, just say the letters you are visualizing, chunk by chunk."*

Buzz: **"T-A-P…T-I-O-N."**

Nanci: *"Excellent. Can you really see the letters?"*

Buzz: *"Yeah. I really can."*

Nanci: *"Let's break, read, and image about ten more words. Then we'll spell some."*

Buzz read ten more words, beginning to process them quite rapidly. Sometimes I miscalled a word and let him be the teacher to find my error—preparing him to monitor (hold and compare) and find his own errors.

"You don't have to write it in the air, just say the letters you are visualizing, chunk by chunk."

Miscalling:

Nanci: *"You're right the word said taption, but you be the teacher and I'll be the student. Help me find my errors. Like what if I said this word says taktion. Did I make an error and where?"*

Buzz: *"You put the letter **K** in where the **P** is. (If using the ADD Program, you may also want to ask for labels.)*

Nanci: *"Right. Let me fix that. What if I say the word says, tiption. Am I right?"*

Buzz: *"No. Tiption. You put an /i/ sound, the letter **I**, in where the **A** should be."*

Nanci: *"Great. If you can correct my errors, you can correct your own. Good on you."*

**Miscalling:
"…You be the teacher and I'll be the student. Help me find my errors."**

Lesson Summary:
Reading and Imaging Two Syllable Words

- Student(s) reads and images two syllable cards, one card changing at a time. Do this only for a short introductory time, or not at all.

   —Be careful to create words consistent with English.

   —Practice open/closed syllable decoding.

- Student(s) breaks, reads and images two syllable words from lists or cards.

   —*Marks* the syllable with a light, diagonal line.

   —*Reads* each chunk, may identify the suffix first, but puts word together front to back.

   —*Images* chunks.

- Practice open/closed syllable decoding.

- Teacher miscalls and student(s) monitors and corrects.

- Do symbol imagery exercises for chunks of the word, specific letters, or whole word (chunk by chunk).

- Use nonsense words to improve phonetic processing.

- Use real words to extend word recognition base.

At the same time that students are practicing reading, the task should be turned to practicing spelling—reading's partner. You will walk back and forth between reading and spelling multisyllable words. My focus has been primarily to develop Buzz's ability to decode, so he can read books—and while reading books extend his spelling lexicon by seeing more and more words. Consequently, Buzz and I often read more than we spelled.

The following lesson demonstrates spelling two syllables, with a slight adjustment in the task and questioning.

SAMPLE LESSON

Imaging and Spelling Two Syllables

The Set

Spelling two syllables.

Nanci: *"Let's practice spelling two syllable words. You'll image and write, chunk by chunk."*

Buzz: "OK. Spelling…huh."

Lesson

Student:
- says word
- counts syllables
- *images word*
- writes word
- breaks word
- checks word

Nanci: *"Right. The words will be nonsense and real, and use the endings you have imaged. Here's the first word, stention. How many syllables?"*

Buzz: *"Stention.* Two syllables."

Nanci: *"Yup. Now say, image, and write each syllable on paper. If you need to, you can make lines for each chunk and then write the word on the line: _____ _____. I don't think you need to, but do it if you want."*

Buzz: "*Stention, Sten…tion.* I don't need the lines, I can spell it. (He wrote **stention**.)

Nanci: *"Great. Now, break the word with one of your diagonal lines."*

Buzz: "Right here." (He broke the word as *sten/ tion*.)

Cover the word and tell me the letters you visualize for each syllable."

Nanci: *"Great. Check what you wrote by touching and saying each syllable. Then cover the word and tell me the letters you visualize in the first syllable."*

Buzz: "*Sten…tion.* Right. **S-T-E-N**. Easy." (He touched and said each syllable, then covered the word.)

Nanci: *"Perfect. Let's do another one. Spell **gargle**, a real word. Say the word, visualize it, and write it."*

"Cover the word and tell me the letters you visualize for each syllable."

Buzz: "*Gargle. Gar…gle.* Easy." (He wrote *gar/gle*, then said and touched each syllable.)

Nanci: *"Excellent. You used one of your endings, **gle**. Perfect. Cover the word and tell me the letters you visualize for each syllable."*

Buzz: "OK. **G-A-R**…**G-L-E**. What does *gargle* mean?"

Nanci: *"Your mom might ask you to gargle warm salt water if you have a sore throat, putting the water way back in your mouth, but not swallowing it."*

Buzz: "Oh…"

Nanci: *"Here's another word. Spell **spection**. Remember, say, image, and write."*

Buzz: "*Spection.* (He counted the syllables then wrote, *spek/tion*.) *Spek…tion.*"

Nanci: *"Right. That would say spection, what else could you have instead of the letter **K**."*

Have student use letters consistent with English spelling patterns.

"Write it with the **C** in it, since if it was a real word it would probably have a **C**."

Buzz: "Well, it could have the letter **C**."

Nanci: *"Yup. Write it with the **C** in it, since if it was a real word it would probably have a **C**."*

Buzz: "Oh, yeah. (He wrote *spec/tion*.) Know what. If you add the little word in, in front it will be the word *inspection*. Hmmm. Spellings not really so hard any more."

Nanci: *"I know. It's great, isn't it. Here's another one. Spell **slashus**."*

Buzz: "*Slashus. Sla…shus.* (Saying and writing each syllable, he wrote *sla/shus*."

Nanci: *"Definitely it sounds just like that. What ending did you visualize that says…"*

Buzz: "Oh…its… (Starting to erase the *shus*.)

189

"...rather than erase that for now, just leave it and write the word another way."	Nanci: *"Wait, rather than erase that for now, just leave it and write the word another way."*
	Buzz: "OK. (Saying and writing each syllable again, he wrote *sla/tious*."
	Nanci: *"Good job. That's using one of your imaged endings. Is there another way you can write that word? Is there another ending?"*
	Buzz: "Oh, yeah. It could be *cious*. (He wrote *sla/cious*.) Which way is right?"
"Is there another way you can write that word? Is there another ending?"	Nanci: *"All of them because this is a nonsense word!"*
	Buzz: "Whew…"
	Nanci: *"As we spell now, I want you to use your imaged endings as much as possible, because real word spelling will use those suffixes. If it was a real word, you'd have to try the two endings and then decide which way looks right, or you'd have to remember a rule, or you'd have to think of a root word to get help, or you'd have to look it up in the dictionary and then visualize it correctly. For example, spell the word **spacious**."*
Have students write phonetic possibilites — then visualize correct spelling.	Buzz: "*Spacious*. Uh, oh. Real word. (Saying and writing each syllable he wrote *spa/tious*.) That's one way. Let me see. Oh, it could also be this way. (Saying and writing each syllable he wrote *spa/cious*.) I don't know which is the real way. I don't think I've seen the word before, but those are the endings I know."
	Nanci: *"You are exactly right, phonetically it could be written either **spatious** or **spacious**. The meaning of the word is lots of space. If you know that space is the root of the word, the core, does that help you guess which way is right?"*

Buzz: "Hmmm. Space. (Eyes up trying to visualize it.) Hmmm. Maybe it's the one with the **C** in it because I think there's a **C** in the word space." (Squinting his eyes and looking at me with a tentative smile on his face.) "It's sure can't be a **T**!"

Nanci: *"Good on you. It is the one with the **C** in it because of the root word space. Now, erase the wrong word, cover the word spacious…and see it and write it in the air. Just like when we practice spelling words on your Visual Spelling Chart."*

Buzz: "**S-P-A…C-I-O-U-S**."

Nanci: *"What's the first letter you see in the last chunk?"*

Buzz: "Can't get me! It's the C!! **C-I-O-U-S**."

Nanci: *"Yup….See how easy this is when you can visualize the letters."*

Lesson Summary:
Imaging and Spelling Two Syllables

- Student(s) spells two syllable words from lists or cards.
  - —*Counts* syllables first.
  - —*Says* the chunks.
  - —*Images* the chunks.
  - —*Writes* the chunks.
  - —*Marks* the syllables with a light, diagonal line.
  - —*Checks* response by touching and saying each chunk.
- Practice open/closed syllable rule.
- Do symbol imagery exercises for chunks of the word, specific letters, or whole word (chunk by chunk).
- Use nonsense words to improve phonetic processing.
- Use real words to extend memorized spelling base.

Practice and Pacing

Practice cannot be once or twice a week, it must be daily. We wouldn't consider having students practice basketball once or twice a week and still expect them to be good basketball players. They need daily practice, we know it and arrange for it. Learning to be a good reader and speller deserves the same consideration.

Daily practice is required to "exercise" the sensory system, like working muscles or eye-hand responses. Practicing reading and spelling multisyllables should be a minimum of twenty minutes a day, but it can extend to as long as four to six hours a day in an intensive therapy environment.

As with the other steps of *Seeing Stars*, overlapping is required to maintain forward progress and keep the lesson energy. The progression for overlapping is: 1) teach a base of suffixes, 2) stimulate imaging sounds/letters at the two syllable level on the Multisyllable Board, 3) overlap to reading and spelling two syllable words, 4) overlap to teaching more suffixes, 5) and while two syllable processing is stabilizing, overlap to teaching prefixes.

Summary

Multisyllable processing is my favorite part of teaching reading and spelling; it is also the part requiring the longest amount of stimulation. Beginning with counting syllables, the multisyllable processing of *Seeing Stars* has three basic components: 1) imaging affixes for instant reading and spelling, 2) imaging and sequencing sounds/letters in multisyllable words, and 3) applying symbol imaging to multisyllable reading and spelling.

It is in multisyllable stimulation that the world of reading and spelling begins to significantly open-up for students. Long Words begin to lose their fearsomeness, and de-mystified, become friends! Sitting across from a fallen goose today, I watched a slow smile come across his face when he realized he had just read one of those Long Words—words *those other kids* could always do. He is definitely mending.

Summary:
Step 9

Imaging, Reading, & Spelling Two Syllables

> **Goal:** To develop symbol imagery for sequencing sounds/letters in two syllable words, and applying that processing to imaging, reading and spelling two syllable nonsense and real words.

1. Counting syllables:
   - Present concept that every syllable has a beat and a vowel letter.
   - Student(s) represents number of syllables by clapping or placing colored squares.

2. Teaching suffixes:
   - Present basic suffixes of le's, ly, tion, ture, ous, etc. to be stored and retrieved through imagery.
   - Suffixes are to be read and spelled instantly.
   - Add the remaining suffixes as appropriate, after beginning sequencing sounds/letters with the Multisyllable Board.
   - See the Appendix for a list of suffixes, or the *Seeing Stars* Kit for suffix cards.

3. Using the Multisyllable Board for sequencing sounds/letters:
   - Present the syllables in a chain, either changing a letter or a suffix.
   - Use chains that focus on changing the letter just prior to the suffix.
   - Student(s) says, images, and writes each chunk on the Multisyllable Board.
   - Do symbol imagery exercises for each chunk.
   - Do symbol imagery exercises for the whole word, chunk by chunk.
   - Be sure symbol imagery is consistent with English spelling rules.

4. Breaking suggestions:
- Present and practice three basic breaking rules:
    — Find and break in front of an ending.
    — Find and break between double letters.
    — Start a syllable with a consonant, if you can.
- Teach the open/closed syllable rule for reading and spelling.
- The vowel says its name if open next to the syllable line.
- The vowel says its sound if closed next to the syllable line.

5. Breaking, reading, and imaging two syllable words:
- Student(s) reads and images two syllable cards, changing one card at a time. Do this only for a short introductory time, or not at all.
- Be careful to create words consistent with English.
- Practice open/closed syllable decoding.
- Student(s) breaks, reads and images two syllable words from lists or cards.
- Marks the syllable with a light, diagonal line.
- Reads each chunk, may identify the suffix first, but puts word together front to back.
- Images chunks.
- Practice open/closed syllable decoding.
- Do symbol imagery exercises for chunks of the word, specific letters, or whole word (chunk by chunk).
- Use nonsense words to improve phonetic processing.
- Use real words to extend instant word recognition base.

6. Imaging, writing, and breaking for spelling two syllable words:
- Student(s) spells two syllable words from lists or cards.
- Counts syllables first.
- Says the chunks.
- Images the chunks.
- Writes the chunks.
- Marks the syllables with a light, diagonal line.
- Checks response by touching and saying each chunk.
- Practice open/closed syllable rule.
- Do symbol imagery exercises for chunks of the word, specific letters, or whole word (chunk by chunk).
- Use nonsense words to improve phonetic processing.
- Use real words to extend memorized spelling base.

7. Teacher miscalls and student(s) monitors and corrects.

Group Instruction

Small or large group instruction does not require changing the steps for two syllable stimulation. Each student has a Multisyllable Board to use, whether in small groups or the entire class. As the teacher says the syllables, students are called on randomly for answers and other students give thumbs up or down to demonstrate their feedback to the response.

Suffix cards can be kept on large cards for group or classroom use, or put on 3X5 cards for each student and kept in individualized plastic index card holders to be practiced for instant reading and spelling. Group lessons can be: 1) teacher says a suffix, students find it in suffix array and hold it up, 2) all students put the suffix card down with one student called on to image, say, and air-write the letters, 3) remaining students give thumbs up or down, 4) all students air-write the letters, 5) teacher holds up the suffix card and all students read it, 6) teacher holds up the card and a designated student reads it.

Reading two syllable words can be accomplished at the chalkboard or on the overhead projector. Break, read, and image as a group or with designated students. Students can hold enlarged core and suffix cards, come to the front of the room and create patterns to be read. Spelling two syllable words can first be done individually within the group, with students saying, air-writing, writing, and breaking at their desks; the writing and breaking can also be done at the chalkboard or on the overhead projector.

Imaging, Reading & Spelling Three Syllables

One day, Buzz came into the Center with a big smile on his face. We'd been imaging and reading/spelling two syllable words in the days previous. Eyes twinkling, with his little squint, he said, "I read a really long word today in class…really long. I saw one of my endings, and I could put the rest of the word together."

Three syllable words are the heart of multisyllable reading and spelling. Though there are numerous two syllable words, students can often memorize them or use contextual cues to guess at them; but, this may not be so with three syllable words. Three syllable words are a threshold point, an opening in the world of literacy. They are 1) more frequent than four and five syllable words, 2) the bulk of the difficulty students have in reading and spelling, 3) usually phonetically consistent (more so than many common words) and 4) usually comprised of prefixes easily processed and memorized. All in all, getting students into three syllable processing is easy, fun, and an important piece in the flight plan.

Imaging Prefixes for Instant Reading and Spelling

Prior to imaging sounds/letters and reading/spelling three syllable words, prefixes should be taught for instant recognition. This is made significantly easier because of their phonetic consistency. Pre, per, pro, por, trans, dis, ex, etc., are not only phonetically regular, but quite short! Present the prefixes on cards, to be read and imaged—the "see and say" technique. Take the prefix away and check for imagery by having the student air-write, *retrieving and identifying a specific letter in the stored imagery*. Once imaged, practice instant recognition and spelling.

S A M P L E   L E S S O N

Imaging Prefixes

The Set

Nanci: *"It's time to learn some beginnings of words, prefixes. If you study the Latin language, you find out that prefixes and suffixes change the meaning of words, but our focus right now is to just learn how to read and spell them. Ready for some beginnings?"*

Buzz: "Yup."

Nanci: *"We'll image them just like we did the endings. First, I'll show you the beginning on a card. You read it, then I'll take it away. You see it, say it, and write it in the air. Easy."*

Buzz: "It sounds like what we did with two syllables."

Lesson

Nanci: *"Right. Here's a really common beginning, prefix. (I show him the **pre** card.) What do you think it says?"*

Buzz: "*Pree*…wait, or maybe it says *pre*." (He says the letter **E** as the /e/ sound.)

Nanci: *"Well, you were right both ways, it can say either pree or pre, with the **E** saying its name or not. So you might have to try two things when you see it or hear it in words. Start with pree. It just has two things for you to try, and you'll be right more often if you say pree. OK?"*

Buzz: "Yeah. That's not so bad. *Pree*."

Imaging Prefixes:

"I'll show you the beginning on a card. You read it, then I'll take it away. You see it, say it, and write it in the air."

198

> Nanci: *"Good. Now, look at it again. And, after I take it away, I want you to see it, say it, and write it in the air, again. (I show and take away the* **pre** *card.)*
>
> Buzz: *"Pree or pre,* **P-R-E**.*"*
>
> Nanci: *"Perfect. See how easy this is? Let's do another one."*
>
> We did a few more prefixes, then I flashed each newly learned prefix card to him, he read and spelled them, doing symbol imagery exercises. Practicing and reinforcing, we added more prefixes as was appropriate.

Lesson Summary:
Imaging Prefixes

- Teacher presents the concept that words have beginnings, prefixes.
- Student(s) images the prefix from the prefix card.
- Student(s) sees, says, and air-writes each prefix.
- Student(s) practices reading and spelling prefixes until recognized instantly.

As students are able to instantly read and spell *some* prefixes, and they are able to image and sequence sounds/letters in *two syllables*, the stimulation is extended to sequencing sounds/letters in three syllable words with the Multisyllable Board. As with two syllables, imaged letters are written on each syllable, this time to include a prefix.

S A M P L E   L E S S O N

Multisyllable Board: Sequencing Letters in Three Syllables

Multisyllable Board at three syllables:

The Set

Nanci: *"Here's the Multisyllable Board again and now we'll use every square for your imaginary letters. Three chunks! The first colored square is for your beginning, the middle is the core, and the last is your ending. You are now in three syllable words!"*

Buzz: "OK…" (Smiling…and squinting.)

"How many chunks do you hear when I say the word *pretaption*? Say the word, feeling the chunks and imaging the letters."

Lesson

Nanci: *"How many chunks do you hear when I say the word **pretaption**? Say the word, feeling the chunks and imaging the letters."*

Buzz: *"Pretaption.* Three. *Pre…tap…tion.* Want me to write the letters on the multisyllable board?"

Nanci: *"Yes, indeed."*

Buzz: **"P-R-E…T-A-P…T-I-O-N."** (He said and wrote imaginary letters on the board, chunk by chunk.)

Nanci: *"What is the last chunk you visualize?"*

"What is the last chunk you visualize?"

Buzz: "Easy. **T-I-O-N.**"

Nanci: *"Right. What's the first chunk you visualize?"*

Buzz: *"Pre…***P-R-E.**"

"What's the first chunk you visualize?"

Nanci: *"You're hot, aren't you. How about the middle chunk? What's the last letter in the middle chunk?"*

Buzz: "Easy. (Eyes up, visualizing.) Hmmm. **T-A-P**. **P**."

Nanci: *"Great! Say, see, and write each of the chunks again, then I'll give you another change."*

Buzz: "Pretaption...**P-R-E...T-A-P... T-I-O-N.**"

"Change *pretaption* to *pretaktion*. Say and touch the old and the new word on the Multisyllable Board."

Nanci: *"Great. Change pretaption to pretaktion. Say and touch the old and the new word on the multisyllable board."*

Buzz: "*Pretaption* to *pretaktion*." (He said and touched each chunk, saying the old and new words.)

Nanci: *"Perfect. Which chunk changed?"*

Buzz: "*Tap* changed to *tak*. **T-A-K.** Wait, or it could be **T-A-C.**" (He said and wrote each chunk on the multisyllable board.)

Nanci: *"Excellent. Either one would say **tak**, but in real words it's probably going to be the letter **C**, so I want you to see it as the letter **C**."*

Buzz: "OK. I have it. **T-A-C.**"

"Either one would say *tak*, but in real words it's probably going to be the letter C, so I want you to see it as the letter C."

Nanci: *"Change **pretaction** to **pretantion**."*

Buzz: "*Pretaction...pretantion.* (He said and touched the board.) Hmmm. *Tac* to *tan*. The **K** changed to an **N**."

Nanci: *"Great. Say and write the whole word."*

Buzz: "Pretantion, **P-R-E...T-A-N...T-I-O-N.**" (He said and wrote on the multisyllable board.)

Nanci: *"Change **pretantion** to **prestantion**."*

Buzz: "Add an **S** at the beginning of the middle chunk. **S-T-A-N.**" (He wrote just the middle syllable.)

Nanci: *"Exactly. Change **prestantion** to **constantion**."*

Buzz: "Easy. *Pre* changes to *con*, **C–O–N**." (He said and wrote just the first syllable.)

Nanci: *"Great. Now say and write the whole word…please!"*

Buzz: *"Constantion.* **C–O–N…S–T–A–N… T–I–O–N**."

Nanci: *"Change* **constantion** *to* **constanly**.*"*

Buzz: "Easy. *Tion* changes to *ly*, **L–Y**." (He said and wrote just the last syllable.)

Nanci: *"Excellent. Excellent."*

Buzz: "So far this is pretty easy."

Nanci: *"You're doing great. What's the second letter you see in the second chunk?"*

Buzz: "Hmmm. The second chunk? *Constanly. Stan.* **T**!"

Nanci: *"Oh my. You're ready to read and spell some three syllables!"*

Buzz: "Mm." (A noise somewhat reminiscent of that grunt-groan from long ago.)

"What's the second letter you see in the second chunk?"

Lesson Summary:
Multisyllable Board: Sequencing Letters in Three Syllables

- Teacher says three syllable words, in a chain.
- Either a letter changes in the core syllable or a suffix changes, but not both.
- Use chains that focus on changing the letter just prior to the suffix.
- Student(s) says, images, and writes each chunk on the Multisyllable Board.
- Do symbol imagery exercises for each chunk.
- Do symbol imagery exercises for the whole word, chunk by chunk.
- Be sure symbol imagery is consistent with English spelling rules.

The level at which students can sequence the letters is the level they can practice application to reading and spelling. Without the ability to sequence the relationship of letters and affixes, students have difficulty monitoring and self-correcting their response to stimulus.

The following lesson has Buzz reading three syllable words, a mixture of nonsense and real. The lesson was done immediately after sequencing letters on the Multisyllable Board.

Reading Three Syllables: "We'll use those cards like we did with two syllables, only now we'll have three parts."

SAMPLE LESSON

Reading & Imaging Three Syllables: Changing one card at a time

The Set

Nanci: *"Now that you know your beginnings—the prefixes—let's practice reading and imaging three syllable words. We'll use those cards like we did with two syllables, only now we'll have three parts."*

Buzz: *"OK."*

Nanci: *"We're only going to do this a little bit, and then go right into breaking and reading."*

Lesson

Nanci: *"Here is a core card, **trep**. I'm going to get one of your endings (**ple**) and one of your beginnings (**ex**) and put them together for you to read. (I showed him the three cards together: **extrepple**.) What does this say?"*

Buzz: *"Ex...trep...ple."* (He touched each card as he said the syllables.)

Nanci: *"Right. (I covered the cards.) Say and write the letters in the air for **extrepple**, chunk by chunk."*

	Buzz: "Easy. *Extrepple,* **E–X…T–R–E–P…P–L–E**." (He said and air-wrote.)
	Nanci: *"Now, I'll change just one card, and you read it for me. I'll take out this card (**ex**) and bring in this card (**dis**). (Now he has distrepple in front of him.) Read it, please."*
Cover the word "Say and write the letters in the air."	Buzz: "Now it says **distrepple**."
	Nanci: *"Right. Say and write the letters in the air."* (I covered the cards.)
	Buzz: "*Distrepple,* **D–I–S…T–R–E–P…P–L–E**." (He said and air-wrote.)
	Nanci: *"What's the last letter in the first chunk?"*
	Buzz: "**S**." (Looking up, he was able to tell me what he saw, *without* having to count each letter out with his hand.)
Breaking, reading, and imaging three syllable words from lists or cards.	Nanci: *"Right again. What might it say if I move this card (**ple**) over to cover up the letter **P**? Like this."* (Now he has **distreple**. I'm wanting to be sure he processes the open/closed syllable rule.)
	Buzz: "The letter **E** is now open, so it says its name. *Distreeple*."
	Nanci: *"Exactly. Now let's do the same only with lists of three syllable words."*
	"Breaking, Reading, and Imaging" three syllable words from lists or cards:
"Here is a list of three syllable nonsense words for you to read. Just like when you read two syllables, break with a light, diagonal pencil mark."	Nanci: *"Here is a list of three syllable nonsense words for you to read. Just like when you read two syllables, break with a light, diagonal pencil mark."*
	Buzz: "OK. Whew."
	Nanci: *"Break and read this word."* (The word is **repanture**.)

"Break and read this word."	Buzz: "There's the **R-E,** *re*. Hmmm. (Breaking the word from front to back, Buzz put in the diagonal lines: **re/pan/ture**.) *Re…pan…ture, repanture.*"
	Nanci: *"Yup. Easy. Tell me the letters you see."* (I covered the word.)
Cover the word. "Tell me the letters you see."	Buzz: "**R-E…P-A-N…T-U-R-E.** *Repanture.*"
	Nanci: *"Excellent. Here's another word to break and read."* (The word is **condition**.)
	Buzz: "*Con…die…tion. Condietion.*" (Breaking as **con/di/tion**, Buzz said /ie/ for the second syllable because the vowel was open.)
Teach the student to flex the vowel sounds.	Nanci: *"Good job. It could say **condietion**, but this is a real word, and you need to be flexible with the vowel, so try its sound /i/."*
	Buzz: "OK. *di…con…di…tion. Condition!*"
	Nanci: *"Right. It's the real word condition. See how you flexed, changed, the vowel sound. That's what you have to do sometimes with real words, sometimes the vowels say their name or their sound. When you are reading in a story, and you get close to a word, the meaning of the word and/or the meaning in the story will help you know what the word is."*
"Sometimes little parts of a word, usually vowels, have to be flexed, changed to a sound or a name, or even just a plain old /u/ sound."	Buzz: "Yeah. I'm already noticing some of that."
	Nanci: *"Right. Sometimes little parts of a word, usually vowels, have to be flexed, changed to a sound or a name, or even just a plain old /u/ sound. And, there isn't anything you and I can do about it, but process words as best we can, and think of a word we know that sounds like that. Now, take a look at the word again, then I'll cover it up, and you image it and write the letters in the air."* (I show him the word **condition** again.)

Buzz: "C-O-N...D-I...T-I-O-N."

Nanci: *"Excellent. Let's break, read and image a few more words, then we'll spell three syllables."*

Buzz broke, read, and imaged ten more words, beginning to process quite rapidly, flexing vowels, gaining confidence. Sometimes we did miscalling, but mostly he broke, read, and imaged.

Lesson Summary:
Reading and Imaging Three Syllable Words

- Student(s) reads and images three syllable cards, changing one card at a time. Do this only for a short introductory time, or not at all.
  —Be careful to create words consistent with English.
  —Practice open/closed syllable decoding.
- Student(s) breaks, reads and images three syllable words from lists or cards.
  —*Marks* the syllable with a light, diagonal line.
  —*Reads* each chunk.
  —*Images* chunks.
- Practice open/closed syllable decoding, and flexing vowel sounds.
- Teacher miscalls and student(s) monitors and corrects.
- Do symbol imagery exercises for chunks of the word, specific letters, or whole word (chunk by chunk).
- Use nonsense words to improve phonetic processing.
- Use real words to extend instant word recognition base into three syllables.

Since reading and spelling are partners in literacy, you can be very comfortable walking back and forth between the two tasks. If your focus is to improve contextual reading first, then give students more words to read than to spell—and vice versa. Here is Buzz, moving immediately into spelling, after having just read three syllables.

S A M P L E   L E S S O N

Imaging and Spelling Three Syllables

The Set

Spelling Three Syllables:

Nanci: *"Let's practice spelling three syllable words. You'll image and write, chunk by chunk, just like you did with two syllables."*

Buzz: *"OK."*

"Here's the first word, *predipment*. Say and write each syllable."

Nanci: *"Here's the first word, **predipment**. Say and write each syllable. You can make lines for each syllable if you want to like this: ____ ____ ____. It's your choice."*

Buzz: *"Predipment. Pre…dip…ment. (Saying and writing each syllable, Buzz wrote predipment on paper, then correctly broke it with diagonal lines, and touched each syllable to check his response.) I don't need those lines."*

"Cover it up, and tell me the letters you see, chunk by chunk."

Nanci: *"Good job. It's perfect. Cover it up, and tell me the letters you see, chunk by chunk."*

Buzz: **"P–R–E…D–I–P…M–E–N–T***."*

Nanci: *"Great. What's the last letter in the second syllable?"*

Buzz: **"P**. *Dip."*

Nanci: *"Perfect. Let's do another one. Spell, **delicious**. Say the word, count the syllables, visualize, write, break, and check."*

"Say the word, count the syllables, visualize, write, break, and check."

Buzz: "*Delicious. De…li…cious.* That's pretty easy, but wait there's two endings that say *shus.* How will I know which one to use?"

Nanci: *"Write it with both endings and then look at both words and see if one looks better than the other. That's what I do when I'm not sure of a word."*

Buzz: "Well, it could be like this." (He wrote *delitious* and then he wrote *delicious,* breaking both words apart perfectly.)

Nanci: *"Yup. It could be either way. Which do you think looks right?"*

"Write it with both endings and then look at both words and see if one looks better than the other."

Buzz: "I can't remember seeing the word very often, but I think maybe it's the one with the **C.** Am I right?"

Nanci: *"Yup. Erase the other one, and take a good look at this one so you can write it in the air, chunk by chunk."* (He erased the errored spelling, looked carefully at **delicious,** and then I covered the word.)

Buzz: "OK. **D-E…L-I…C-I-O-U-S.**"

Nanci: *"Great. Now write it again on paper so I know the right way is in your mind, not the wrong way! You never know when you might want to spell that word in a story, and I don't want it stored in your mind wrong!"*

"Erase the other one, and take a good look at this one so you can write it in the air, chunk by chunk."

Buzz: "I've got it." (He wrote *delicious.*)

Nanci: *"Great. Say a sentence with that word in it, just so I'm sure you know the meaning of it."*

Buzz: "I'd like a delicious ice-cream cone right now!"

Lesson Summary:
Imaging and Spelling Three Syllables

- Student(s) spells three syllable words from lists or cards.
  — *Counts* syllables first.
  — *Says* the chunks.
  — *Images* the chunks.
  — *Writes* the chunks.
  — *Marks* the syllables with a light, diagonal line.
  — *Checks* response by touching and saying each chunk.
- Practice open/closed syllable rule.
- Do symbol imagery exercises for chunks of the word, specific letters, or whole word (chunk by chunk).
- Use nonsense words to improve phonetic processing.
- Use real words to extend memorized spelling base.

With practice and daily reinforcement, Buzz began to easily read and spell three syllable words, and on into four and five—accurately imaging and sequencing the letters and affixes. We practiced every day, sometimes lots of nonsense words to reinforce sequencing letters in multisyllable words, and sometimes lots of common multisyllable real words to expand his sight vocabulary. The multisyllable stimulation extended and expanded his Auditory and Visual Circles; the Auditory Circle expanded because of increased automaticity in three syllable processing, and the Visual Circle expanded because of increased word recognition.

Four and Five Syllables...and the Schwa

While words in English can go as high as seven or more syllables, the multisyllable stimulation of *Seeing Stars* is focused on *three* syllables because of the preponderance of three syllable words in reading and spelling, especially in common usage. Teaching students to accurately read and spell three syllable words takes care of much of their literacy needs, allowing for oral vocabulary and contextual cues to fill in some remaining gaps. Further, it has been my experience that processing three syllables is a threshold point in that when students reach automaticity with this task, they often very easily reach mastery in four and five syllables.

Although not as crucial as three syllables, extending students into four syllables is strongly advised, providing more experience with even longer words and the schwa. English has primary and secondary accent in words, and while accent is not as pivotal as other aspects of processing words, it does help to know about an unaccented syllable and the schwa. Briefly, the schwa is when a vowel letter makes the /u/ sound in an unaccented syllable. In a word like *president,* for example, the middle syllable is not accented so the vowel is not stressed and thus a clear vowel sound is not easily heard. It becomes an /u/ sound, a nothing kind of sound where your tongue is in a medial position.

In spelling, if Buzz only had phonetic processing to rely on for processing a multisyllable word, the schwa could cause him frustration and many low spelling scores, just as it did Jan the college student. But, since Buzz has learned to "symbol image" words, the newly functioning part of his sensory system aids him in dealing with the schwa because he can visually remember parts of words. In reading, the schwa is not such an issue because Buzz can use his oral vocabulary or contextual cues to help him read the word; he may be unaware that he is flexing accent or vowel sounds.

When the student's sensory-cognitive processing becomes automatic and comfortable with three syllable words, extending into four and five easily uses the established phonemic awareness and symbol imagery base. The Multisyllable Board is extended to four syllables simply by imaging two syllables on one square, or taking the imagery to the air without the use of the board. Keep in mind, that it is not productive to ask students to image a multisyllable word in its wholeness. Our image screen may not fit the entire word, but it can fit the word syllable by syllable, chunk by chunk. When extending into four and five syllables, either in the air or on the board, ask for the *Visualizing and Verbalizing* to be syllable by syllable.

Summary

Establishing three syllable imaging, reading and spelling is a milestone, a threshold point, in phonetic processing, symbol imagery, decoding, and spelling. Prefixes and suffixes are imaged, stored, and retrieved for instant reading and spelling. Long Words are being conquered. Following the breaking rules for three syllables, applying prefixes and suffixes, four and five words really do become little words put together, and can be read and spelled with a fair amount of ease. Symbol imagery exercises continue to build an important aspect of sensory-cognitive processing, with the exercises carefully applied to each syllable in the multisyllable word, rather than the entire word.

Summary:
Step10
Imaging, Reading & Spelling
Three Syllables

> **Goal:** To develop symbol imagery for sequencing sounds/letters in three syllable words, and applying that processing to imaging, reading and spelling three syllable nonsense and real words.

1. Teaching prefixes:
   - Present basic prefixes of pre, pro, con, dis, ex, trans, etc., to be stored and retrieved through imagery.
   - Prefixes are to be read and spelled instantly.
   - Add the remaining prefixes as appropriate, after beginning sequencing sounds/letters with the Multisyllable Board.
   - See the Appendix for a list of prefixes or the *Seeing Stars* Kit for prefix cards.

2. Using the Multisyllable Board for sequencing sounds/letters in three syllables:
   - Present the syllables in a chain, either changing a letter or an affix, but not both.
   - Use chains that focus on changing the letter just prior to the suffix.
   - Student(s) says, images, and writes each chunk on the Multisyllable Board.
   - Do symbol imagery exercises for each chunk.
   - Do symbol imagery exercises for the whole word, chunk by chunk.
   - Be sure symbol imagery is consistent with English spelling rules.

3. Breaking, reading and imaging three syllable words:
- Student(s) reads and images three syllable cards, changing one card at a time. Do this only for a short introductory time, or not at all.
- Be careful to create words consistent with English.
- Practice open/closed syllable decoding.
- Student(s) breaks, reads and images three syllable words from lists or cards.
  — Find and mark the syllable with a light, diagonal line.
  — Image chunks.

4. Imaging, spelling and breaking three syllable words:
- Student(s) says, images, spells three syllable words.
  — Student counts syllables first.
  — Student may need to write each syllable on a designated line for extra support.
  — Student follows the pattern of: say, image, write, break, and check.
- Do symbol imagery exercises for chunks of the word, specific letters, or whole word (chunk by chunk).

Group Instruction

Small or large group instruction does not require changing the steps for three syllable stimulation. Each student may have a Multisyllable Board, whether in small groups or in the classroom. When the teacher says the syllables, students are called on randomly for answers and other students give thumbs up or down to demonstrate their feedback to the response.

As with the suffix cards, prefix cards can be kept for the group, on large cards for classroom use, or also put on 3X5 cards for each student and placed in individualized plastic index card holders to be practiced for instant reading and spelling. As with suffix stimulation, small and large group practice for instant recognition of prefixes requires group management, keeping the lesson interesting and focused on the task of imagery and reinforcement. Flash the prefixes for group reading since prefixes are easier and shorter than suffixes; but, it is important to call on a "Buzz" to image the letters, ensuring his participation and development.

As with two syllables, reading three syllable words can be fun at the chalkboard or on the overhead projector. Break, read, and image as a group or with designated students. Students can hold enlarged core and affix cards, come to the front of the room and create patterns to be read. Spelling three syllable words can first be done individually within the group, with students saying, air-writing, writing, and breaking at their desks. The writing and breaking can also be done at the chalkboard or on the overhead projector.

19

Integration to Contextual Reading

With multisyllables conquered, and an expanded sight vocabulary, Buzz was becoming different. His brown eyes had a different look, he even appeared taller. I'd recently observed him stop and talk with other students. Though his original diagnostic testing indicated high scores in oral language comprehension, oral vocabulary, and following oral directions, and he always got the point of conversation and humor, he had seemed shy and reserved in social and academic settings. This had changed. Buzz was different now.

In the beginning with me, Buzz had stiffened and looked tortured when requested to read a paragraph during his initial diagnostic evaluation. Brave, however, he had done what was asked of him. Beads of perspiration had formed on his upper lip when he was asked to spell word after word on the initial spelling test. But, he had spelled anyhow. His bravery was also extended to school, where he had sometimes been asked to read aloud, enduring the snickering of other kids; or when he had been asked to leave the room for his special class or had been given medication with the eyes of other children on him. Through it all, Buzz had been a small, courageous little boy, still taking the spelling tests in school, still going to the library during library time (no matter that he couldn't read the books at his level), and still making an effort despite a gnawing pain that perhaps he wasn't very smart. Still padding along through life.

Well, smart he was—as he now knew. Getting to this point had taken a short snippet out of the gestalt of his life, just a few months. Every day, we had read and spelled multisyllable words, always imaging them. Every day, we had moved more words from his Turtles to his Jets. Every day, he did symbol imagery, and when his sight words began to increase, we began reading on the page to integrate and apply his new skills from the Auditory and Visual Circles to the *Language Circle*.

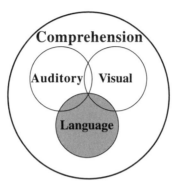

As we turned our attention to developing the Language Circle, Buzz began the integration of reading in context, short paragraphs at first, then pages and finally a book. Words on the page. The majority of what we decode is decoded in context; and when decoded accurately and fluently *with comprehension*, we are *reading*. Contextual reading is fluent decoding with comprehension and interpretation.

Developing contextual reading requires an integration of sensory-cognitive processes and skills—phonemic awareness, symbol imagery, concept imagery integrated with oral vocabulary, word attack, and word recognition. This act of integration is quite a feat, really. The Reading Circles are an easy way to conceptualize it because you can think of the underlying processes and skills of the Auditory, Visual and Comprehension Circles now being *applied* and *practiced* to develop the Language Circle. Beginning with the Auditory Circle spilling into the Visual Circle, one Circle spills into another and another allowing them all to develop and expand. In the past, we have made the mistake of assuming processing and skills in the Auditory and Visual Circles, and initiated reading instruction in the Language Circle by putting books in front of children and asking them to read. This doomed many children to failure and frustration unless they, by genetic chance, were gifted the underlying sensory-cognitive processes that allowed them to develop the other Circles on their own. The children given the phonemic awareness and symbol imagery gene—or the concept imagery gene—were the children anyone could have taught to read because they arrived genetically wired to perceive sounds, image letters, and image concepts. It was, and is, the other children who need direct stimulation to develop all the Circles *and learn to integrate them*.

This last step of *Seeing Stars* integrates the Circles for fluent contextual reading. The act of integrating sensory-cognitive processing and skills, though simple to conceptualize, is quite profound, requiring conscious and directed practice—daily reinforcement—to be sure new skills aren't frightened away. How many times have you witnessed an exodus of processing when your students read on the page? How many times have you seen children know a word out of context, but in context miscue it into a wild guess? Those sensitive word recognition and/or word attack skills that scuttled away at the sight of sentences and paragraphs can be taught to integrate with comprehension for fluent contextual reading, but they need nurturing and direct encouragement.

The first nurturing issue is when to begin contextual reading and with what material. Using the Reading Circles as your guide, begin the overlap into contextual reading when the Auditory and Visual Circles are *starting* to develop, don't wait until they are completely developed. Reading in context provides decoding practice and reinforcement of sight words, and thus continued stimulation of the Auditory and Visual Circles. However, don't start the overlap too soon and frustrate your student. A base of sight words and phonetic processing in at least single syllables is the rule. With the "when" determined, initiate the act of reading on the page with short paragraphs rather than full pages of context. Those sensitive new skills may indeed scream and run away when they see a whole page or a number of pages to read, especially if the reading is to be aloud and performance expected. Choose short material at an easy reading level, not a frustration level.

Once the decision for when and what is made, before putting the student on the page, it is important to understand the role of the Comprehension Circle in reading in context; it can be another cause of decoding errors—the scuttling. While accurate, fluent decoding is the goal of the Language Circle, the Comprehension Circle is the end result; and, it also interacts with contextual fluency. The act of reading has one primary purpose: to get meaning. Our instinctive goal, yours and mine, in decoding on the page is to get meaning, to comprehend, to learn, to enjoy. As we read, we make meaning from the words by imaging the concepts the words form, and we self-correct our decoding from discrepancies in that imagery. Sometimes as our mind naturally gravitates to this making of meaning from language, we skip words or change words and decoding errors occur.

The making of meaning and imagery is the same natural goal for our students, except for those with weakness in concept imagery and, thus, a comprehension deficit. Those students may just read *words*, in-one-ear-and-out-the-other the words go. Those students have difficulty imaging parts to whole so they end up just mouthing words, consequently, reading may not be interesting to them or easy, even though decoding may be a breeze. The book, *Visualizing and Verbalizing for Language Comprehension and Thinking*, identifies concept imagery—the ability to create a gestalt (whole)—as the primary cause of this language comprehension weakness. Since the book provides specific steps to develop concept imagery, we won't spend further time here discussing comprehension issues, though it is of passionate concern to me. Instead, we will assume concept imagery and focus on strategies to develop fluent, confident, accurate decoding to be integrated with comprehension. The demonstration lesson in this chapter assumes concept imagery is intact, which in fact it was for Buzz.

Directing and Questioning in Context

With the appropriate material in hand, the Auditory and Visual Circles developing, and no underlying weakness in concept imagery, contextual reading and your directing role begin. While students are learning to integrate sensory-cognitive processes and skills, decoding errors will occur; and handling those errors appropriately provides stimulation toward the integration.

Your students must read for comprehension. Teach them to read for imagery/meaning rather than to read to decode squiggles. Your first question in cueing a decoding error is, *"What does that make you picture?"* rather than *"What does that word say?"* In the latter, who noted the decoding error, you or the student? Right. You noted the error by drawing attention to a specific word. But, in reality, with independence the goal, who needs to note the error? Who will be interacting with print to get meaning? Right. Students need to note the error; so, the age-old method of pointing to a decoding error does not facilitate self-correction and independence. Just as the act of decoding requires monitoring and self-correction, the act of reading in context requires monitoring and self-correction. In contextual reading the monitoring comes from 1) sensory input from oral vocabulary and concept imagery for gathering meaning, and 2) sensory input from phonemic awareness and symbol imagery for decoding accuracy. All the Reading Circles are now interacting to facilitate monitoring, self-correcting, and independence.

After your first question directs students' to the *gestalt* (imagery/meaning), your next question directs them to the *part*, the errored word. For decoding errors, as discussed previously, respond to the response by helping students compare their response to the stimulus, noting the discrepancy, and correcting the processing. This is very well presented in the ADD Program where responding to the response is covering the word and asking students what they felt for a specific part of the word, thus stimulating the matching of articulatory feedback to print. In *Seeing Stars*, responding to the response is covering the word and asking students what letters they imaged for a specific part of the word, thus stimulating the matching of symbol imagery to print. In any case, avoid telling students the correct word and moving on. While this facilitates fluency for the moment, it can be a false economy. It is worth the time to question appropriately to direct the application and monitoring.

Miscalling Small Words

With questioning to imagery first on your list of contextual directing, and responding to the response second, you may also need to provide extra stimulation for the application practice. If students miscall small words such as *if*, *the*, *and*, etc., the miscue isn't usually caused by a decoding deficiency, rather it is usually caused by decoding speed and attempts to get meaning. In trying to decode for meaning or fluency, students such as Buzz may still be slow in recognizing words instantly; thus, they read the surface structure of print quickly in an effort to look good or get to the deep structure of meaning and imagery.

In our attempts to develop fluent contextual reading, we have many parts of the gestalt to keep in mind. For example, although decoding accuracy may be the goal, we must be careful about correcting, calling attention to every decoding error because it may send the message that reading is decoding, not comprehending. If your student is a new reader, trying very hard to read fluently, let a few of the small errors go for awhile, and come back to them later when he or she has learned to enjoy reading and imaging concepts. If your student has had years of negative experience with reading on the page, such as an adult dyslexic or a child like Buzz, he or she may be experiencing much anxiety; again, let a few of the small errors go until some confidence and enjoyment begins to occur from reading. On the other hand, if your student has no trouble getting meaning and always reads to understand, then a focus on decoding accuracy is appropriate. Carefully chose when and when not to focus on decoding accuracy; while it does provide imagery for meaning, it is a *part* needing to be placed in a *gestalt*.

If correcting miscalls must be a focus, directly stimulate the missing monitoring by setting up a miscalling activity—you miscall, students correct. You misread a sentence and they find the error. They become the teacher and receptively monitor your errors, preparing them for monitoring their own when reading independently.

Contextual fluency can also be facilitated by identifying specific words to decode prior to reading in context. This has been done for years in many classrooms where students are presented terms to decode and understand, but it can be very helpful in remedial situations. When Buzz started into contextual reading, his eyes pleaded for clemency. Many times, I took words from the paragraphs he was going to read and used them for symbol imagery practice. By decoding them first, he was storing them in imagery for retrieval; fluent reading of the paragraph was facilitated because he didn't have to stop and phonetically process quite so many words. While helping to increase his fluency, it also helped increase his sight words, little by little spilling over into increasing his self-confidence and self-image.

The following lesson is with Buzz reading in context after he had learned a few hundred sight words and had begun to process two syllable words quite well. I might have started the overlap sooner, but his sessions were moving along quickly in the basic processes and I knew his first experiences in context needed to be very positive. He was facing the dragon. It was here he had experienced much pain with reading. It was here his bag of cognitive skills needed to be a little bit bigger before he picked up the s**w**ord.

S A M P L E   L E S S O N

Integrating and Applying Processes to Contextual Reading

The Set

Nanci: *"Guess what. Today we're going to read some paragraphs. It's time to put some of your new skills together—your sight words, your two syllable processing, your good imagery skills. Do you visualize when you listen to someone read?"*

Buzz: "What do you mean? Like see pictures in my mind?"

Nanci: *"Yes. Like picturing and sort of making your own movie."*

Buzz: "Yeah. I do that. I especially do it when I hear a story, or when someone else reads to me."

Nanci: *"Good. I thought so, but I just wanted to call it to your attention, because as you read this paragraph, that is the first thing I want you to do. Think about the images the words create for you."*

Buzz: "OK…"

Lesson

This is the short paragraph Buzz would read: The little boy had a very small white mouse in his pocket. He got it at school. He wanted to take it home and put it in his room. But, he was afraid of what his mother might think. He thought he might be given another lecture about not bringing home stray animals.

Nanci: *"Read this to me."*

Buzz: *"The little boy had a very tall white mouse in his pocket."* (He read rather slowly, especially on

"Let's stop after that sentence and see what that makes you picture."

"Since those images don't make sense, go back and read every word carefully to be sure we have the right images."

"Remember, words create images. When you're reading and the images don't seem right, go back and check the words you read. Read the next sentence."

the word "mouse" and "pocket" but he got through the sentence.)

Nanci: *"Let's just stop after that sentence and see what that makes you picture."*

Buzz: "Well, it's kind of strange. I see a tall mouse in his pocket, but it doesn't make sense. How can the mouse be tall and still be in his pocket?"

Nanci: *"Exactly. Since those images don't make sense, go back and read every word carefully to be sure we have the right images."*

Buzz: *"The little boy had a very tall…Oh, the word is* small, *a very small white mouse in his pocket.* That makes more sense! I can picture that. A boy with a little white mouse in his pocket, wiggling around."

Nanci: *"Great picture. Remember, words create images. When you're reading and the images don't seem right, go back and check the words you read. Read the next sentence."*

Buzz: *"He got it at school. He wanted to take it home so he could put it in his room."* (Buzz misread 'so he could put it in' for the words <u>and put it in his room</u>.)

Nanci: *"Good, keep going."* (I decided to let the decoding errors go because it was Buzz's first time on the page, meaning wasn't interrupted, and my goal was to build his fluency and confidence for the task. I had plenty of time to get at decoding accuracy.)

Buzz: *"But, he was afraid of what his mother might think. He thought he might be given another lection about not bringing home stray animals.* (He read slowly but accurately, until he got to the word *lecture*.) Hmmm. Something doesn't sound right there. (He started to go back, but frustration and fear set in. I needed to help him decode.)

Nanci: *"Let's just check this word. (I covered the word, lecture.) When you say lection how many chunks do you have?"*

Buzz: *"Lection. Two."*

Nanci: *"What letters do you visualize for the last chunk, the last syllable?"*

Buzz: "Shun. Shun. Oh, yeah. That's T-I-O-N."

Nanci: *"Right, let me show you the word again and see if that matched."* (I uncovered the word, lecture.)

Buzz: "No, that's T-U-R-E. Chur. Lec...chur. Lecture. Oh, I've got it now."

Nanci: *"Great. Now read the whole sentence over again, so you can put it together with those images."*

Cover the word "lecture." "Let's just check this word. When you say lection how many chunks do you have?"

Practice and Pacing

Daily practice and appropriate questions are necessary to develop the integration of processing for fluent contextual reading. As usual, an overlapping of steps is necessary, and the cue to overlap is some proficiency in the Auditory and Visual Circles. As stated earlier, when students can process a simple syllable with imagery, and have established a number of Jets, overlap them into contextual reading at an easy reading level. As their processing increases in symbol imagery and a sight word base is expanding, increase the level and amount of time spent reading in context. Always keep the big picture in mind that contextual reading is an integration of processes. If your students are excessively slow in contextual application, and the level of reading is appropriate, the Auditory and Visual Circle may need more development. In other words, you may have overlapped too soon into context. If this is the case, time would be better spent developing phonetic processing and symbol imagery for word attack and sight words, rather than reading in context.

Summary

Contextual reading is an integration of all the Circles; and the act of integrating can be facilitated by questioning imagery to language—whether concept imagery for comprehension or symbol imagery for decoding.

Buzz was overlapped into contextual reading as the Auditory and Visual Circles were developing and expanding. Daily reinforcement began to yield accuracy and fluency on the page. As two syllables stabilized, he was extended into three syllables, his sight words continued to increase, and we spent more and more time integrating his skills and applying them into contextual reading.

One day, having previously moved him from third to fourth grade level material, I moved him to a fifth grade book. His very grade. His eyes looked at me. He took a deep breath and smiled. Without fear, he read accurately, integrating his ability to get meaning with his ability to monitor and self-correct his decoding errors. He read fluently at his grade level! When he left that day, wounds and wings nearly healed and mended, I thought I saw him stop and look up to the sky.

He's Back in the Formation

It was seemingly a day like any other when Buzz came into the room. Other children (some young and some old, but children nonetheless) were in treatment sessions, some doing the ADD Program, some doing the V/V program, some doing both, and many doing symbol imagery. Small and large voices were doing lip poppers and tip tappers and tracking sounds with blocks for the ADD program. Voices were saying, "Here I saw…" for the V/V program, and animatedly gesturing their concept imagery. Small and large hands were writing letters in the air for the *Seeing Stars* program. Voices were saying letter names. Backwards and forwards they went, prefixes and suffixes shooting in the air like stars in the Universe. And, there stood Buzz looking at me. The time was getting close. Today was his last day. Today was the day I had to say good-bye…

He was gleaming again, as he had for many days now. He'd just gotten another 100% on his spelling test, including the challenge words. He was able to easily read his fifth grade history, health and English books. He sat down and looked at me. A small hand went into his backpack and brought out a new book. A hard book, with Long Words.

"I got this at the library. I went to a harder section of books, and I think I can read it. I'd like to try. I…I…want to because you said it was your favorite book."

Tears started to form, those dreaded tears. Struggling for him not to see my eyes, I looked down at the book he was showing me. Oh my.

Taking a deep sigh, I opened to my favorite part and said, "Lets try this little part right here and see how it goes."

Buzz started to read, with fair ease: "When I pointed to him his palms slipped slightly, leaving greasy sweat streaks on the wall, and he hooked his thumbs in his belt.

A strange small spasm shook him, as if he heard fingernails scrape slate, but as I gazed at him in wonder the tension slowly drained from his face. His lips parted into a timid smile, and our neighbor's image blurred with my sudden tears. 'Hey, Boo,' I said."

I looked at him, wiping an eye, "You can do this, Buzz. You can do anything." We went back to the beginning of the book and he started, *"When he was nearly thirteen my brother Jem got his arm badly broken at the elbow. When it healed, and Jem's fears of never being able to play football were…"*

Buzz read for quite a long time, then all too soon the session was over. When we closed the book, it seemed as if only Buzz and I, Scout, Jem, and Atticus had been in the room. Looking at me, he took his new book, and put it back in his backpack. Then he loaded his 100%-spelling-test in his binder, and stuffed his "stuff" in his backpack. Head down. Quiet. Then he looked at me again and said, simply, "Thank you."

Getting up, amongst the lip poppers and tip tappers, images and hands in the air, Buzz and I went to the door.

The time was here. It was time to let Buzz go. I knew I probably wouldn't see him again, and if I did he might be old. Or worse, I might be old, and perhaps he'd gasp when he saw me or not recognize me at all. Part of me wanted him to stay, so I could greet his little brown eyes everyday and watch as they learned. But, a part of me, a bigger part, wanted him to go, to fly into the formation with his other geese, fly along for awhile until he got all his strength back, until his wings were very, very strong and he was confident.

When I said good-bye to him that day, I thought there was a chance now that he might even be a lead goose someday. And as he started around the corner, he stopped for a moment, and looked back at me. Then he turned and left. I could have sworn I saw him fly.

The Summary

21 Seeing Stars & the ADD Program

The ADD Program and *Seeing Stars* are pals working on the sensory system, one, two, three—friends working toward a common goal. Both programs work on a *part* of the reading and spelling process and both contribute mightily to the whole, but alone, neither are the whole. Neither the ADD Program nor *Seeing Stars*, are the answer to teaching children to *read* and *write*. But, the ADD Program and *Seeing Stars* together are an answer in teaching children to *decode* and *spell*. Got it? I'm sure you do by now!

For those of you unfamiliar with the ADD program, we help students *discover* and *label* articulatory feedback, the sensory input from their mouth. The questioning process to stimulate articulatory feedback develops that first step of sensory-input needed for monitoring (needed for self-correction and ultimately independence). *Labeling* the sensory-input with language creates imagery while describing the sensory-input. For example, the label "lip-popper" (for the phonemes /p/ and /b/) describes the feeling *and the imagery of* that sensory-input. *The ADD Program labels are direct stimulation of cognitive dual coding—the integration of imagery and language.* Once the dual coding is developed for individual phonemes, the consonants and vowels, the ADD Program applies the sensory-input to sequencing phonemes in syllables. Students use little colored blocks to track sounds in syllables, simple and complex. This develops the hold and compare process of monitoring response to stimulus. As tracking sounds is establishing, students are overlapped to encoding and decoding tasks of nonsense and real words, extending into multisyllables.

For many years, I traveled around the country teaching classes in the ADD Program. Those were the days when I came home to three children wondering where on earth their mother went nearly every weekend. Those were the days of returning late on a Saturday evening to water dripping from the kitchen ceiling, and giggles ringing down the staircase from two little boys splashing and sliding in the upstairs bathroom. Those were the days when the ADD

Program and I were doing battle against the psycho-linguists cry for only good literature in the hands of children.

We have been very good friends for a very long time, ADD and I. I contributed to some of its steps, particularly multisyllable color encoding and error handling techniques; I took it with me to fight many battles about the need for phonemic awareness and word attack skills; I cried when it wasn't accepted; I screamed in frustration about the lack of understanding of it and the importance of the Auditory Circle; ultimately I developed the Venn diagram out of my love of the ADD Program and that frustration. The ADD Program is wonderful. I have not abandoned it. Integrating *Seeing Stars* into the ADD Program is an important step in helping to move phonemic awareness into symbol imagery—it's home. And, vice versa. Integrating the ADD Program into *Seeing Stars* is important in helping those students with severe weakness in phonemic awareness be able to verify phonemes. Integrating the two programs together is positive for both, and here is a step by step example for you.

1. Integrate Imaging Letters step with ADD Program consonants and vowels.

Begin the integration of *Seeing Stars* into the ADD Program at the phoneme/grapheme level—the consonants and vowels. As students are learning the sound, label, and letter of phonemes, also teach them to image the letters and air-write them—the Imaging Letters step.

2. Do the Imaging Syllable Cards step prior to, or in conjunction with, ADD Program Color Encoding.

Before students begin sequencing phonemes and articulatory feedback with the blocks, exercise their symbol imagery by having them *see* letters in syllables, image and air-write—the Imaging Syllable Cards step. Needless to say, begin the stimulation at the simple level and move into complex, just as you would with blocks. Strengthening symbol imagery will assist your students with the hold and compare necessary in tracking the old and the new pattern in ADD Program blocks because the old pattern will be imaged and thus stored and retrieved more easily. How many times have you had students say to you, "What was the old pattern? Can you say it again?" Trust me, I know. This will help you and them.

3. Integrate <u>Imaging</u> <u>and</u> <u>Sequencing</u> <u>Syllables</u> into the color encoding step of ADD.

As students are color encoding, tracking with blocks and *using* articulatory feedback, teach them to write imaginary letters on the blocks while saying the letter name. It won't interrupt the students' attention to articulatory feedback if you monitor that they are feeling and labeling fairly well. *Have the student write the letter on the block and say the letter name, **after** he or she has labeled the sound.*

4. Do the Syllable Board along with color encoding step of ADD.

Do the Syllable Board even if you are doing the ADD Program. Writing imaged letters on the board is another reinforcement of symbol imagery, even though your student may be writing imaged letters on the blocks.

5. Do <u>Imaging</u> <u>and</u> <u>Sequencing</u> <u>Syllables</u> as a separate step from ADD.

Have students image and write in the air, *with* and *without* chains, while you are having students do color encoding and one syllable encoding and decoding in the ADD Program. Keep the symbol imagery stimulation moving to strengthen their monitoring and self-correction. It is very important to do this step *along* with ADD.

6. Integrate imaging and sequencing of multisyllables with ADD multisyllable color encoding.

If you are using ADD felts and blocks for tracking sounds at the multisyllable level, have students write imaged letters on the blocks and say the letter name rather than the label when the sound/letter changes. Also have students say and write imaged letters on the prefix/suffix felt as it changes, or have them write letters on the whole word at any time during the task. In conjunction with this, use the Multisyllable Board for more symbol imagery stimulation and reinforcement.

7. Integrate symbol imagery into all decoding and encoding tasks of the ADD Program.

Have students visualize and verbalize, image and say the letters they read or spelled, whether in single or multisyllable words. For example, in the ADD Program, if you had students decode a word with the tiles, cover the word and have them tell you the letters they saw. If decoding a single syllable word on a list or card, cover the word and have them tell you the letters they saw. If decoding a multisyllable word, cover the word and have them tell you the letters they saw, syllable by syllable, but not the whole word. You are stimulating their symbol imagery by having them retrieve what they saw and recreate it with verbalizing. Another way to think of that is that you are directly stimulating their dual coding by having them visualize and *verbalize* the letters.

Spelling requires the same use of imagery. If you have asked students to spell a word, integrate imagery into the task prior to having them represent the word with tiles or print. For example, if you ask students to spell a nonsense word with the tiles, first ask them what letters they imaged, have them write the letters in the air, and them show you the letters with the tiles or vice versa. This is applicable from one through multisyllable words. In multisyllables, first have them visualize and verbalize the suffix, or a prefix, or an accented syllable, then have them spell the word in print.

8. Error Handing with Seeing Stars and ADD Program

Both programs respond to the students' response, as do all Lindamood–Bell instructional programs. For *Seeing Stars* and ADD, because they are both developing phonemic awareness and decoding/encoding, use imagery and labels interchangeably. For example, if correcting an error in the *Seeing Stars* step of sequencing letters on the Syllable Board, ask the student to feel and label. If correcting an error in the color encoding step of ADD, after the student has labeled a sound, have him or her image the letter.

Integrating *Seeing Stars* and ADD will be easy for you once you have the big picture that the sensory system works together in that oh-so-ingenious fashion of integration. It doesn't compete and neither should we. We must be honk, honk, honking at each other for support and encouragement, congratulating ourselves on the lift we provide and a journey well traveled. Have you read that last chapter, yet?

Summary & Theories

Here is where I say good-by to you, just in case you did read the last chapter first. Before I go, and leave this routine of four AM coffee (decaf), stocking feet, the beep of the computer turning on while it's still dark outside, and cats in the courtyard scratching at the window of the French door, I want to give you an idea of some of the research that supports what you have read and learned in this book. Believe me, I'd rather toss out the two bins of articles, books, and papers, but a few of those "you's" out there may be honkingly anxious to read theory. I've loved and respected you too in writing this book, or I'd be heading for the beach right now.

Reading is an integration of processes resulting in comprehension and interpretation. The gestalt or whole of reading is comprehension; the part of reading is decoding. Reading words, the parts, and bringing those parts to whole, results in cognition—thinking, analyzing, interpreting, reasoning from language.

Imagery is the Cognitive Foundation for Words and Concepts

The best description of cognition, what it takes for our brain to think, whether from oral or written language, whether with words or concepts, is Allan Paivio's Dual Coding Theory (DCT). Paivio (1986) stated, *"Cognition is proportional to the extent that language and mental representations (imagery) are integrated."* In other words, when we think, either understanding words or concepts, we dual code with imagery and language; and, our *ability* to think is dependent on, or proportional to, how well we integrate the two processes. This integration, dual coding, is necessary for connecting to language concepts and language symbols; it is necessary for reading comprehension and decoding/spelling words.

Decoding and comprehension skills interact with one another during reading. Accurate and fluent print-based decoding skills provide a needed basis for good reading comprehension, and good comprehension skills allow students to make correct inferences about the identity and meaning of many words in text (Stanovich, 1991).

However, neither decoding or language comprehension can be assumed, and comprehension skills seem to be diminishing as is noted in numerous recent studies. For example, the National Assessment of Educational Progress (NAEP) findings have shown particular deficiencies in higher-order reasoning skills, including those necessary for advanced reading comprehension. "Reading instruction at all levels must be restructured to ensure that students learn to reason more effectively about what they have read," states the report, which showed such a drastic and "baffling" decline in the reading comprehension performance of nine- and seventeen-year-olds that the report was delayed for five months while researchers refigured the statistics and reexamined the test items. Dr. Jane Healy noted in 1990, "Despite a serious effort on the part of elementary and high schools to beef up the curriculum, students of all ability levels show virtually no gains in higher-order skills.... Tests which show that young children's scores are rising may simply be focusing on the 'lower level' skills of word reading while neglecting the real heart of the matter: How well do they understand what they have read? Can they reason—and talk, and write—about it?" And this weakness in comprehension extends into higher levels as the College Board recently noted, "Even among students who can *read*, verbal skills have declined on the Scholastic Aptitude Test (SAT)." These comments are why I am so passionate about the need for attention to the comprehension of language, and the foundational domino of imagery.

Imagery is a sensory-cognitive skill basic to both oral and written language comprehension. Though the relationship between imagery and cognition has been discussed for many years, it is the *integration* of imagery with language that makes Paivio's theory so compelling. However, as far back as Aristotle imagery has been discussed in relation to thinking. In his contemplations on the ability to reason, Aristotle theorized that *man cannot think without mental imagery*. Along with Paivio and Aristotle, there is very strong historical evidence regarding the role of imagery in cognition. Jean Piaget (1936, cited by Bleasdale 1983) wrote that over time, schemata become internalized in the form of imaged thought. Proceeding chronologically to examine more interesting research and historical commentary, note Arnheim (1966), "Thinking is concerned with the objects and events of the world we know…When the objects are not physically present, they are represented indirectly by what we remember and know about them. In what shape do memory and knowledge deliver the needed facts? In the shape of memory images, we answer most simply. Experiences deposit images." Words and concepts deposit images. Experience with isolated words, parts, creates images, and experience resulting from integrating those parts to whole creates images. We dual code.

Kosslyn (1976) conducted a developmental study on the effects and role of imagery in retrieving information from long-term memory. He reported that imagery provided significantly more opportunity for retrieval. Linden and Wittrock (1981) stated, in a study with fourth graders, "the generation of verbal and imaginal relations or associations between the text and experience increased comprehension approximately by *fifty percent*." Further research by Oliver (1982), in three experiments to determine if an instructional set for visual imagery would facilitate reading comprehension in elementary school children, concluded, "These findings indicate that teachers should try to help children develop the metacognitive skill of visual imagery as a strategy for improving comprehension…Visualization enhances comprehension." The research of Long, Winograd, and Bridge in 1989 provided further evidence regarding the role of imagery in reading: "Our results suggest that imagery may be involved in the reading process in a number of ways. First, imagery may increase the capacity of working memory during reading by assimilating details and propositions into chunks which are carried along during reading. Second, imagery seems to be involved in making comparisons or analogies— that is, in matching schematic and textual information. Third, imagery seems to function as an organizational tool for coding and storing meaning gained from the reading." Imagery assists with processing both words and concepts, the parts and the whole.

The nineties have produced further research to support the role of imagery in cognition and reading. "Imaginative processes, including imagery and emotional responses, are necessary to breathe life into the reading experience," Sadoski (1992). Sadoski, in researching DCT, reading theory, and reading efficiency, noted that imagery is directly related to reading comprehension, reading recall, and verbal expression. He has validated Paivio's DCT in numerous studies involving imagery, comprehensiveness, and recall by carefully proving that the more reading concepts are imaged the better they will be comprehended, the longer they will be recalled, and the more interesting they will be to the reader.

What part of the brain is used for imaging, how large is the screen, and many questions concerning the phenomena of imaging can be answered by reading any of Stephen Kosslyn's books. For example, in *Frontiers in Cognitive Neuroscience*, edited by Kosslyn and Andersen, Farah's (1984) work is reported. "Examination of the lesion sites in this subset of patients implicated a region in the posterior left hemispheres as critical for the image generation process. The analysis also provided evidence that the long-term visual memories used in imagery are also used in recognition, and that dreaming and waking visual imagery share some underlying processes." In *Wet Mind*, Kosslyn and Koenig also report very interesting information regarding imagery's role in reading. "The best clues about what different parts of the brain are doing during reading come from PET studies. These PET studies indicate that even reading single words is a complex activity, which involves several different parts of the brain. In particular, reading has a visual component and an associative memory component. The visual component clearly appears to involve the preprocessing and pattern activation subsystems, given the locus of the activation, and the associative memory component appears to involve the categorical property lookup subsystem."

The Interaction of Phonological and Orthographic Processing in Contextual Fluency

Decoding is a part of the whole critical to contextual fluency and comprehension; the Auditory and Visual Circles are subsets of the greater set of comprehension, and frequently referred to as the phonology and orthography of decoding. Decoding requires phonological processing for word attack skills and attention to the orthography of words, their print representation. No more than a few years ago, the theorists were still arguing about the cause of deficits in decoding and whether decoding words were even necessary in reading. However, correlational and causal research spanning more than a twenty-five year period, has recently diminished some of the debate. Difficulty in segmenting phonemes within spoken syllables and words has been documented as the primary factor in problems in the word attack aspect of reading. You know this as the Auditory Circle. This neurophysiological processing problem has been called *lack of auditory conceptual function, phonological awareness, and phonemic awareness* by various researchers (Calfee, Lindamood & Lindamood, 1973; Liberman & Shankweiler, 1985; Lundberg, Frost & Peterson, 1988; Olsen, Forsberg, Wise & Rack, 1994; Wagner, Torgesen & Rashotte, 1994; Torgesen, Wagner & Rashotte, 1996).

Awareness of the segmental structure of words, *as an oral language skill,* is critically related to acquiring an understanding of the alphabetic principle: how letters can be used to represent words on the printed page. Although various studies have shown traditional phonics training to be effective in helping students to understand the alphabetic principle and develop independent word reading skills (Adams, 1990; Ball & Blachman, 1991), a common problem with many of the training procedures reported in the research is that they may not be powerful enough to aid students who are most at-risk for the development of reading difficulties. For example, both Torgesen, *et al* (1992) and Lundberg (1988) found that a significant number (20-30%) of the least able students were unable to profit from phonics training procedures. This is because typical phonics activities assume ability to say a word indicates ability to identify its individual sounds. In reality, studies indicate that 20-30% of the population lack adequate development of this sensory-cognitive function (Calfee, Lindamood & Lindamood, 1973; Shankweiler & Liberman, 1989).

Though phonological processing is a cornerstone of word attack, and word attack a necessary piece of word recognition, word attack and word recognition can be thought of as separate functions supporting one another, integrating with meaning. Oliver, (1967) said, "If the child can hear the separate sounds within words and learn what letters represent these sounds he is ready to build his sight vocabulary by word study which emphasizes phonics, look-say, or a combination of both approaches. We might think of each word analysis factor as providing another strand with which the beginning reader may weave a perceptual net in which he can catch, scrutinize and hold unfamiliar words. It gives him a way to really look at a new word, analyze it, visualize it, and commit it to memory."

Berninger (1986) assessed orthographic skills and their relationship to oral reading. "The combination of a measure of phonemic (phonological) coding <u>and</u> a measure of letter-cluster (orthographic) coding accounted for 64% of the variance in oral reading of single words and 71% of the variance in silent reading of single words at the end of first grade. The measure of the letter cluster coding explained an additional 9% of the variance in oral reading and an additional 7% of the variance in silent reading beyond that explained by the phonemic coding measure alone."

Barker, Torgesen, and Wagner (1992) discussed the role of orthographic processing skills in different reading tasks. "Current models of word identification processes (Barron, 1986) suggest that the information involved in identifying words from print falls within two broad domains: phonological and orthographic." Their study provided evidence regarding individual differences in the ability to form and store orthographic representations not accounted for by differences in nonverbal IQ, phonological ability, or reading experience. The most important finding from their initial analyses was that the contribution of orthographic skills varied significantly depending on whether children were reading isolated words or text. "The substantially stronger relationship of orthographic ability to the text reading measures suggests that fluent access to visual word representations plays a special facilitative role in the reading of connected text. The mechanism of this facilitative effect seems likely to involve processes unique to the sequential processing of written words. If, as suggested by Frith (1985), orthographic skills enable automatic recognition of words as wholes, than those with more strongly developed orthographic representations should have a special advantage in performing complex operations such as textual processing."

To the question of decoding versus use of context cues, in second, fourth, and sixth grade readers, Simons and Leu (1987) report results generally consistent with recent work by Stanovich (1980) and others who emphasize the importance of automatic context-free word recognition ability. "Our data seem to suggest that models of the reading process will need to be expanded to explain variation in using graphic and contextual information in response to the constantly changing contextual richness in texts."

Harris and Sipay also wrote about the needed interplay between word attack and word recognition. "There is growing evidence that either pathway may be utilized, with the choice depending on various factors (Haines & Leong 1983). Novice readers may be more reliant on direct access when reading familiar words (Katz & Feldman 1981), or when they have been instructed through a whole-word method or have had little instruction and practice in decoding (Barron 1981a). Research strongly supports the position that direct access is possible for skilled readers, but that they use a mediated access when confronted by unknown words (Kleinman & Humphrey 1982). Word familiarity has a significant effect on lexical access and language processing. A word's syntactic and semantic complexity does not affect the time it takes to access it in the mental lexicon. A word's phonological or orthographic organization as well as its relation to other words in the lexicon may influence access time (Foss, 1988)."

That we can measure phonemic awareness with an instrument as precise as the LAC Test is a contribution to the field of education, and this same preciseness is needed in measuring imagery as related to processing symbols and concepts. At Lindamood-Bell, we have been using the Visual Attention Span for Letters (VASL) subtest of the Detroit Tests of Learning Aptitude as a measure of symbol imagery. Individuals are shown a sequence of random letters. After the stimulus is removed, the individual *says* each letter he or she remembers, in the order given. While the test has old norms, it is a method of measuring symbol imagery since the individual *sees* and *says* from a given stimulus. A recent analysis noted a high correlation between word recognition skills and performance on the VASL for 229 students receiving treatment in our Centers.

Summary

For many years, when the ADD Program and I were on-the-road in battle fatigues, I heard the statement that there was no one thing needed for every one in reading. The statement "teach to a strength" was and is telling educators to ignore weaknesses (more than likely because they don't know how to develop them) and teach to the students learning style, implying that literacy can be gleaned from one source or another. Frankly, this is nonsense. Reading and spelling require an integration of specific sensory-cognitive processes, and every reading/spelling act requires these same processes. Further, the need for these processes in reading and spelling doesn't discriminate on the basis of gender, ethnicity, socio-economic status, or age. We simply have to integrate processes, one function cannot compensate for the others if independence is the goal.

Processing language is a parts-whole issue. The words are the parts, the concepts are the whole. Each of our sensory-systems has to bring the specific sensory-cognitive functions to the task of processing language and thinking. Symbol imagery is a part of the whole with an important direct relationship to phonemic awareness, word attack, word recognition, spelling, and contextual fluency.

We need to better fight the continuing literacy wars—disputing whether or not decoding words is an important aspect of reading, and whether or not to teach children to spell. We need better ways to directly measure the relationship of imagery to cognition, both parts and wholes. We need better ways to measure oral language processing and critical thinking. But, until then let logic prevail—identify and stimulate sensory-cognitive processing skills and integrate those parts to the whole. As the practitioners of education, let's fly down and help as many fallen Buzzes as we can.

I must go now. The sky is calling.

The Story Of the Geese

Life isn't about just living, it's about making the journey really count. Geese do that. Here's their story, a lesson for all us humans flapping and honking through life.

I heard this story from Sue Nichols, a Kindergarten teacher in Florida. Sue used it in a motivational speech, integrating her experience with five year olds and the story of geese. Teaching Kindergarten was my first teaching experience and one of the highlights of my life. Little faces, eager and earnest, had a zeal and love for life that was a delight for me to meet everyday. Being on the floor with five year olds as one of the characters in creative dramatics or marching around the room in a rhythm band was a wonderful way to start a career in education—and perhaps one of the reasons Sue's story touched me. Being lucky enough to be with little children all day is being lucky enough to be with individuals in a natural state of loving and learning.

Here is a paraphrasing of Sue's story of the geese, integrated with the innocent eyes of her kindergarten children.

> Sue had just graduated from college and married the man she "had chased for most of my teenage years." They were sent to Germany where she was asked to be the Kindergarten teacher at a NATO school, a very small school on a mountain side in Germany. She took the opportunity and looked into the eyes of thirty-six five year olds.

> "In those days we didn't have terms like hyperactivity, dysfunctional family, attention deficit disorder, all the 512 things we have now to beat to death mothers and fathers in parent conferences. I hadn't heard of the drug Ritalin. It was a long time ago, and my thighs were firm. I had only heard of Bayer Aspirin and Penicillin. That was the extent of my drug culture. But, I did know that

when my children got real restless and weather permitting, we would go outside and lay in the short grass of the German mountain side and look up in the sky. We would look at the clouds and make up stories. And, while looking at the clouds and making up our stories, the most beautiful geese would fly by and they would honk, honk, honk.

"The kindergarten children and I thought the geese were honking at us on the ground and we would give them names. The children looked forward to watching and naming the geese.

"My husband, being scientifically minded, made me look up lots of information on the geese. The more I learned the more I could see that the way geese lived represented heroism, leadership, responsibility, focus, momentum, positive outlook, persistence. So here is the story of the geese. Through the years, I have blended a little of the scientific evidence of the geese with the excitement and focus of my kindergartners.

"*Lesson #1*: The flapping of each birds wings creates an uplift for the birds that follow. By flying in a V formation, the entire flock adds 71% greater flying range than if a bird flew alone.

"*The Kindergarten lesson from that is:* If we share in a common direction and a sense of community, we will be going quicker and we will be going easier because we are traveling on the thrust of one another.

"*Lesson #2*: Should a goose ever fall out of the V formation, it suddenly feels the resistance and the drag of flying alone. If you are watching you will see him or her get back into the V formation to take full advantage of the lifting power of the bird immediately in front.

"*The kindergarten lesson:* If we have as much sense as the goose we will keep in our V formation with those who share our vision and are headed where we want to go. We will be willing to accept their help as well as give our help to others.

"Lesson #3: When the lead goose gets tired, it rotates back into the formation and another fresh goose flies at the point position.

"The kindergarten lesson: As with the geese, we are interdependent upon each other. It pays to take turns when you are doing the hard tasks and when you are sharing the leadership.

"Lesson 4: The geese weren't honking at me and my kindergartners, they were honking, honking, honking, up to the lead goose congratulating him or her on flying fast and strong.

"The Kindergarten lesson: We need to make certain that all of our honking, honking, honking from behind is encouraging and never ever something else.

"Lesson 5: When a goose gets sick, or wounded, or shot down, two geese always drop out of the formation, one on each side, and take the sick and wounded goose down to the ground to protect it. They stay with the goose, never leaving it until the goose becomes well again or dies.

"The kindergarten lesson: If we have as much sense as a goose, we too will stand by each other in the difficult times as well as when we are strong. Remember we are all sparks in a glorious fire."

All the children and adults you work with can benefit from the energy and effort you put into learning to stimulate symbol imagery. Literacy is an integration of processes, an integration of parts to whole, and symbol imagery is a critical part of that whole.

Any individual can teach this, and any individual can learn to fly. Buzz was a spark in our glorious fire. Today he's a lead goose. You can do this. You can do anything.

Appendix

The Appendix

Sample Syllable Cards

The *Seeing Stars Kit* includes 25-50 Syllable Cards at each level, but the following are examples to illustrate how you can make them for yourself. If you do make them, put them on 3X5 cards, printed in lower case letters, and use spelling patterns. (Mine will be better…)

VC:	CV:	CVC:	CCV:
ap	ti	pait	pli
oaf	sha	teab	ska
eam	pi	male	gri
id	pea	lafe	sni
ot	fe	fesh	shru
oob	dee	sheb	flai
eek	cho	vec	sma
ane	bou	cib	qui
ait	wi	burb	klu
ope	lu	jeck	dw

VCC:	CCVC:	CVCC:	CCVCC:
isp	sleck	misk	blaift
oint	kruck	foint	glorked
outs	quip	barsp	twoamp
urst	plaim	timp	fresp
ilk	smare	bubbed	quepped
eshed	trube	geft	blebd
aint	sleem	poant	treaft
esp	preth	deats	cresp
echt	thrup	dax	sloict
oosp	clep	peft	tremp

Using the Chains

There are ten changes in the following chains of nonsense and real words, single through multisyllable. The purpose of this stimulation is twofold: 1) to develop and stabilize phonemic awareness with symbol imagery, and 2) to begin the transition to English spelling patterns. Real words are for fun…and to let students know this is a meaningful exercise with some purpose in the real world!

The chains include spelling patterns such as ai, oa, ea, and may have an addition or an omission that will change the structure of a chain. You can ask for the variations to be imaged, such as ain, ane, aen, or a C for a /k/, an "ed" for a /t/, /d/ depending on the level of your students.

Each chain will not show all the possibilities for a pattern, you can stimulate that as appropriate for your students needs. A plural or past tense can change the sound of a letter. For example, *mobs* is written with the letter **S**, but sounds like the letter **Z**. *Mopped* ends in "ed" but sounds like a /t/ and *mobbed* ends in "ed" but sounds like a /d/. When doing these chains, have the student write what they hear, but finish with appropriate English spelling patterns; or if a real word, the final version must imprint accurate spelling.

These chains may or may not be enough for your students. You can create many more depending on the needs of your students. You can do this. You can do anything.

VC

ip	av	ooth	eef, eaf	ope
ap	ev	oth	eeth	oat, ote
af	iv	ith	ath	oak
ag	ouv	ath	aith	ov
og	out	ash	ave	iv
ob	ouch	atch	ov	av
os	ooch	itch	oj	am
om	ooth	in	on	um
osh	uth	an	an	ut
och	ath	on	een, ean, ene	ute

VC

ok, oc	uf	if	ag	op
ol	uth	ip	ig	ep
osh	uck	ib	ish	ip
om	um	id	in	ap
on	un	oid	ib	up
en	oin	ood	ij	um
ain	out	oos	ip	ush
an	oudge	ook	ap	udge
oon	oug	oon	ep	un
in	ig	on	eth	ain (aen, ane)

VC

op	ib	out	ak, ck	idge
ep	ab	eat	ick	adge
etch	am	eaf	uck	edge
atch	an	each	eck	odge
itch	ag	eam	ock	udge
otch	egg	am	ot	um
utch	esh	oom	op	up
up	etch	em	osh	ip
ul	atch	aim	otch	idge
us	itch	oim	off	adge

VC

oim	os	etch	ick	eaf
oin	og	esh	ack	ean
on	osh	ash	uck	ain
an	ock	ap	um	an
ap	on	ab	un	in
ape	an	ib	oun	oan
ipe	in	id	ouf	oaf
epe	oon	idge	outh	oof
ene	oof	udge	oul	ooch
in	ool	adge	oil	atch

CV

ti	ga	li	je	ri
te	gu	la	ji	ra
ta	zu	le	ja	ro
va	ze	fe	cha	tho
vo	zi	fou	na	wo
vi	zoo	pou	tha	wa
shi	boo	shou	za	wee
chi	ba	shoi	zoi	see
chu	na	sha	zou	sa
thu	noi	cha	mou	cha

CV

moo	te	ki	na	ve
moy	ti	li	ne	vi
mi	tay	pi	fe	voo
ri	ta	poe	foy	too
ji	sa	zoa	fu	koo
ja	se	zu	wu	roo
cha	su	za	lu	ro
sha	lu	ze	li	co, ko
tha	mu	re	le	mo
tho	bu	che	lee,lea	lo

CV

te	si	wi	je	se
se	ci	pi	ji	ge
see	ce	ti	ja	gi
fee	le	ta	va	gu
fo	fe	ra	ve	lu
jo	fa	ri	vi	nu
mo	ta	ro	vo	ni
sho	sha	rou	lo	ki
cho	shoi	tou	ho	ko
tho	choi	zou	how	ke

CV

thi	hu	wa	te	sha
tho	pu	ta	se	da
thu	pi	sa	soi	va
ru	li	da	loi	ba
re	le	fa	zoi	na
ri	re	fi	zou	ne
zi	ra	gi	dou	noi
vi	roo	li	jou	soi
mi	zoo	pi	joi	goi
moo	koo	vi	noi	goo

CV

fe	di	pe	ke	te
te	da	pi	ki	ti
ti	de	po	ko	ta
too	fe	lo	koe	cha
ta	fa	sho	toe	che
ga	ba	le	joe	le
goo	va	re	je	li
goy	cha	ri	ji	ki
joy	la	ra	gi	ka
je	lu	wa	ge	sa

CV

fou	ti	ne	mi	se
gou	ni	ni	mo	si
jou	ne	di	sho	su
dou	ke	ri	zo	sa
di	ze	ro	zoo	ta
de	fe	po	moo	sha
da	se	pa	too	shi
ra	ke	ba	te	mi
re	koy	sa	ne	li
fe	toy	ka	le	le

CVC

teb	fip	zop	noop	pit
tab	pip	zap	noon	sit
tub	pep	zash	nooth	git
sub	pup	sash	booth	got
sush	lup	sish	bath	gosh
such	lap	sesh	tath	mosh
much	lep	sep	tam	mom
moich	lip	nep	tan	vom
moit	sip	nap	tin	voom
toit	ship	nip	tib	boom

CVC

lej	des	kib	jib	sif, cif
luj	tes	sib	jab	saf
lun	tesh	seb	jeb	zaf
nun	ten	neb	jub	zef
noin	tef	noib	cub	zouf
nin	fef	noin	cuth	zoum
nine	fif	coin	cath	zeem
line	fife	coith	can	seem
shine	life	toith	fan	seek
shan	pife	teeth	fain, fane	keek

CVC

map	kish	rep	teap	tat
lap	kif	rap	leap	tet
lip	kife	rup	feap	set
lop	pife	pup	fap	fet
lock	pipe	pum	faf	fat
leck	pape	pun	fafe	fatch
neck	pap	lun	safe	latch
nep	zap	lan	same	batch
sep	zep	lin	sam	bash
ses	zel	lean	sat	bab

CVC

cap	ped	sid	tez	toon
cag	led	did	tiz	zoon
gag	fed	nid	ziz	soon
gig	fad	ned	zez	sun
gog	gad	nad	zaz	chun
gom	dad	nan	zap	chup
gum	dade	noin	nap	chap
gume	dame	noun	nip	chan
fume	lame	noup	noip	chain
fum	tame	poup	poip	chin

Complex Syllable Chains

VCC

asp	est	oofs	aimz (s)	ekt, ect
amp	east	oops	amz	ept (ed)
omp	eapt (ed)	ooks (x)	amp	opt
omd	opt	ox	oimp	orpt
ogd	okt, oct	ex	oisp	urpt (ir,er)
ogz (s)	act	ax	oips	ipt
ovz	aft	afs	eps	ift
oovz	ast	als	ips	aft
oobz	ats	alt	isp	ast
oomz	oats	ilt	imp	ats

VCC

oupt	oapt (ed)	oifs	ips	omz
ouct	oaps	oiks	ifs	ogz
ousht	aps	oips	oafs	ogd
usht	ops	oisp	afs	ovd
ust	ols	asp	ats	ivd
uts	olj (ge)	isp	ast	izd
its	ulge	ips	oist	idz
ifs	ilge	eaps	oits	imz
iks (x)	alge	eafs	oiks	ibz
ex	ald	eans	oisk	igz

VCC

oikt	aimp	ojd	ogd	isp
oist	aimd	ond	ovd	ips
east	aivd	ind	avd	aps
ast	aivz	and	ivd	asp
ats	aigz	end	ijd	amp
aps	agz	und	ajd	amd
asp	anz	uvd	and	azd
osp	ans	ujd	ond	avd
ops	ats	und	eand	ovd
oops	ast	ound	ead	odd

VCC

ex	apt	ets	uzd	unch
ax	ant	est	udz	unt
ox	oint	oist	idz	usht
ops	ount	oift	izd	uft
oops	ouct	oifs	oizd	eft
oips	oult	oufs	oidz	eaft
oiks	alt	afs	oigz	east
oisk	olt	aps	oinz	eats
oist	ult	asp	oinch	eafs
oits	ust	isp	inch	oafs

CCV

sti	gri	fla	tro	sku
sta	fri	fra	trou	slu
sla	pri	dra	crou	spu
swa	pli	dwa	clou	swu
sna	sli	swa	cle	twu
sni	spi	sla	cre	twe
sne	spee	sle	bre	tre
sle	stee	ple	ble	gre
gle	snee	pre	sle	cre
fle	see	pri	spe	cle

CCV

sna	snee	gli	snea	twi
snai	stee	gri	spea	swi
sne	swee	fri	slea	swa
sle	spee	fro	sloa	swoa
ble	spe	frou	smoa	swoa
blu	ske	froi	smo	swee
bru	swe	broi	smi	twee
tru	dwe	droi	sme	tree
twu	dre	dwoi	smu	gree
swu	de	swoi	swu	gre

CVCC

nejd	camp	mosp	melk	neft
nezd	casp	moisp	milk	nefs
noozd	calp	moist	misk	nels
nouzd	palp	moits	musk	nelb
noudz	pulp	mets	must	belb
doudz	gulp	sets	muts	bulb
dougz	shulp	sest	tuts	chulb
doumz	thulp	seft	tust	chuld
doimz	thusp	left	toist	chuzd
moimz	thump	weft	toast	chudz

CVCC

loups	joint	belk	roips	gost
poups	joist	belt	roisp	gots
pousp	joits	felt	roimp	jots
tousp	joiks	fest	romp	jets
toust	joils	fets	pomp	jest
touts	joips	fefs	pump	nest
bouts	poips	fafs	pulp	nept
bets	poisp	nafs	pulk	neft
best	hoisp	naks	sulk	teft
test	hoist	fax	culk	tet

CVCC

daft	zist	lest	siogz	bizd
gaft	zits	lets	sougz	bezd
gaift	zoits	leks	soudz	beld
gaist	zouts	leps	souvz	belt
waist	zoots	lesp	soumz	telt
west	zoost	lelp	soumd	test
wets	zust	loolp	sound	tets
weps	zast	poolp	pound	toots
wesp	zats	pulp	pond	toits
zesp	tats	pup	pobd	toist

CVCC

misp	kelk	juts	vizd	bibd
mips	kelf	just	vidz	bivd
maps	shelf	jupt	vadz	bivz
masp	melf	junt	vazd	bimz
mask	milf	junch	vald	mimz
task	milk	lunch	valt	migz
cask	tilk	launch	vast	tigz
cast	tilt	naunch	last	toogz
cant	tist	nench	lant	toigz
coint	tint	nelch	land	goigz

CCVC

glof	grum	draf	flep	pred
grof	glum	drag	flap	prep
groif	blum	dwag	floup	pren
gloif	slum	kwag	sloup	prem
sloif	scum	quag	snoup	brem
spoif	swum	quat	snout	brim
skoif	swim	quit	swout	blim
snoif	slim	quif	sweet	blime
smoif	slime	queef	skeet	blame
stoif	spime	queech	speet	bame

CCVC

sked	smade	groit	browl	frip
skoid	slade	gloit	broil	prip
sloid	slate	glot	froil	plip
snoid	skate	gloat	foil	plep
swoid	scat	float	sfoil	slep
stoid	scath	flat	stoil	skep
stoit	slath	flate	snoil	swep
stot	slash	fate	snail	sweep
stout	stash	sate	snait	sneep
state	statch	skate	snit	skeep

CCVC

twub	dwan	grub	snush	tradge
twun	dwin	glub	stush	bradge
trun	twin	glud	swush	badge
frun	twine	glup	skush	bladge
fun	swine	glep	slush	bledge
flun	spine	glip	blush	sledge
flaun	spife	plip	brush	slidge
flin	slife	ploup	bruch	sidge
slin	sife	sloup	bruj	ridge
swin	skife	spoup	brudge	bridge

CCVC

snap	blad	clef	plop	breb
snep	bleed	cref	plup	brev
skep	sleed	cresh	plud	blev
skip	slud	crish	plug	slev
skipe	snud	crush	prug	spev
stipe	stud	trush	proog	spep
stape	swud	trash	ploog	spap
slape	swus	brash	sloog	spape
snape	skus	bran	snoog	spade
snap	snus	brain	swoog	spad

CCVCC

thrust	crisp	slips	bleeps	tricks
thrist	craisp	slits	breeps	trucks
thrits	craisk	slats	broaps	trups
thrips	fraisk	slast	broats	prups
trips	frusk	slaist	froats	praps
traps	frosk	slaisp	froast	traps
trasp	frost	scaisp	floast	trasp
troisp	prost	swaisp	floats	brasp
troist	prots	sweesp	cloats	brusp
treast	props	sweeps	cloafs	brup

CCVCC

slaps	clips	drips	flaps	spent
scaps	clisp	drops	fleeps	spant
scasp	clasp	drocks	freeps	spast
scusp	claps	drucks	freesp	scast
scust	clups	drusk	froasp	scalt
swust	crups	trusk	croasp	spalt
swist	croaps	trunk	croast	spilt
twist	croaks	trink	croaft	spist
twits	cloaks	shrink	craft	spits
tweets	clucks	shrank	claft	spats

CCVCC

trouts	skips	swelk	bramp	grouts
troust	skaps	stelk	broimp	groups
trouft	staps	stilk	broimd	grousp
traft	stats	stisk	broigd	glousp
draft	stast	swisk	broizd	gousp
drift	steast	swiks	broidz	pousp
droift	sleast	swips	droidz	prousp
froift	fleast	spips	drodz	presp
froint	feast	spisp	dodz	preps
troint	beast	spoisp	bodz	peps

CCVCC

snald	klijd	shruzd	blanch	ceft
swald	kwijd	shrudz	branch	cleft
swalk	quijd	drudz	brunch	clest
sweelk	quid	dridz	drunch	clets
sweelt	quit	drizd	drulch	slets
sweet	quite	drigd	grulch	sleats
sweest	quike	drid	gulch	sleaks
sweets	quick	drind	glulch	speaks
seats	quip	dwind	glutch	speaps
meats	quiep	dwint	clutch	smeaps

Two Syllable

aply	faption	stepture	troply
iply	fiption	skepture	tropture
oply	fiction	skecture	topture
option	ficture	slecture	tosture
iption	fisture	slection	tasture
iction	finture	sleption	pasture
action	fanture	septure	papture
acture	fanly	sention	pepture
anture	fafly	nention	penture
vanture	fifly	vention	venture

Two Syllable

fecture	blapture	praction	biggle
lecture	blasture	traction	bliggle
lacture	blature	tration	liggle
lapture	slature	trament	giggle
lasture	slasture	trapment	gigle
sasture	slasly	tropment	giture
sasly	skasly	cropment	gature
saptive	skusly	cropture	nature
captive	skudly	crocture	snature
cantive	skufly	crosture	snative

Two Syllable

swikly	drosly	saptive	spasture
swakly	drisly	captive	sasture
smakly	dristure	cantive	sastion
smaction	fristure	canture	saption
smuction	frusture	carture	saply
smuption	frupture	parture	saptive
smupture	frupment	sparture	santive
smulture	grupment	scarture	stantive
smusture	gripment	slarture	staptive
stusture	gipment	slature	stapment

Two Syllable

trection	fipment	spuply	gargle
traction	fapment	stuply	garble
tractive	tapment	stupture	garment
traptive	taptive	stusture	gament
trapment	saptive	stesture	sament
trament	gaptive	stecture	stament
tracious	gantive	stecment	station
tacious	gative	stepment	snation
sacious	gacious	slepment	nation
spacious	gracious	slement	nature

Two Syllable

twoption	noidly	fumble	mecture
troption	noinly	frumble	mection
treption	coinly	trumble	meptio
trection	cointure	tumble	peption
trention	mointure	stumble	pleption
trenture	moisture	stumly	plention
tresture	masture	stuply	plection
presture	casture	stuption	plecture
prasture	crasture	stuntion	plesture
pasture	cracture	suntion	presture

Three Syllable

transmitly	refebly	persnection	consteption
transmiply	rebebly	consnection	constection
transmipment	rebably	conspection	constrection
promipment	rebadly	inspection	construction
pormipment	rebaply	inslection	construption
premipment	rebapture	insleption	constuption
permipment	rebasture	insteption	constupture
permiption	rebanture	instention	constulture
perniptoin	rebalture	perstention	prestulture
promiption	prebalture	prestention	prestusture

Three Syllable

disprective	perdantion	redeptive	untricial
disprentive	perdrantion	receptive	untrecial
disprenture	perdwantion	recentive	untrecious
disprelture	exdwantion	recenture	unprecious
dispresture	exdantion	recentle	unpretion
conpresture	expantion	concentle	unprention
conprepture	expaption	conpentle	unprenture
conpreption	expaply	conpenture	inprenture
conprection	expadly	conpepture	inprelture
conpection	conpadly	conpecture	misprelture

Three Syllable

dishenture	unropment	reventure	transmakly
prehenture	unripment	misventure	transmatly
prehenly	exripment	misvanture	transmasly
preheply	expripment	misvacture	transmasture
prehesly	exprepment	misvapture	dismasture
prehesture	expreptive	convapture	dispasture
prehasture	exprentive	conventure	displasture
prehature	exprective	adventure	displesture
perhature	exprection	adventive	displesly
perfature	expreption	inventive	replesly

Three Syllable

permitly	intrepment	conjadly	condalment
permatly	intepment	conjedly	conpalment
permaply	distepment	conjenly	conpalture
permaption	distepture	conjenture	conpeltlure
permeption	distepcious	conjecture	conpulture
permection	distecious	consecture	conpusture
permention	disticious	consesture	dispusture
transmention	desticious	presesture	dispunture
transmection	deslicious	prosesture	dispucture
transmiction	delicious	presenture	dispupture

Three Syllable

predepment	prodiction	continly	repepment
predepture	prediction	continture	repedment
predecture	predection	conticture	repedly
predenture	predrection	contricture	repesly
condenture	predrention	contripture	repesture
condepture	disdrention	contristure	dispesture
transdepture	disdention	protristure	dispenture
transdecture	disdeption	protrasture	expenture
transdacture	disdaption	protranture	expecture
transdanture	disdaction	protrapture	expection

Affixes

The following are *some* of the common affixes. (See the ADD Program *Suffix Grid* for an excellent way to organize many regularly irregular suffixes.)

Prefixes			
re	por	ex	mis
pre	con	con	un
pro	dis	de	
per	trans	non	

Suffixes			
le's	ture	ment	cial
ly	ous	tive	tial
tion	cious	sive	al

1000 Instant Words
by Edward Fry

The following three hundred words are reprinted from *1000 Instant Words, The most Common Words for Teaching Reading and Spelling* with permission from Dr. Fry. These words are the most common words in English use, and *they make up 65% of all written material.*

the	or	will	number
of	one	up	no
and	√ had	other	way
a	by	about	could
to	word	out	people
in	but	many	my
is	not	then	than
you	what	them	first
that	all	these	water
it	were	so	been
he	we	some	√ call
was	when	her	who
for	your	would	oil
on	can	√ make	now
are	√ said	√ like	√ find
as	there	him	long
with	use	into	down
his	an	time	day
they	each	has	did
I	which	√ look	√ get
at	she	two	√ come
be	do	more	~~made~~ make
this	how	write	may
have √	their	√ go	part 9/22/10
from	if	√ see	over

270

new	great	put	kind
sound	where	end	hand
✓take	✓help	✓does ᦁ᧐	picture
only	through	another	again
little	much	well	change
✓work	before	large	off
✓know	line	must	✓play
place	right	big	spell
year	too	even	air
✓live	mean	such	away
me	old	because	animal
back	any	turn	house
✓give	same	here	point
most	✓tell	why	page
very	boy	✓ask	letter
after	✓follow	went	mother
thing	came	men	answer
our	✓want	✓read	✓found *find*
just	✓show	✓need	study
name	also	land	still
good	around	different	✓learn
sentence	form	home	should
man	three	us	America
✓think	small	move	world
say	✓set	✓try	high

every   ✓left   until   idea
near   don't   children   enough
add   few   side   ✓eat *ate*
food   while   feet   face
between   along   car   watch
✓own   might   mile   far
below   ✓close   night   Indian
country   something   ✓walk   real
plant   seem   white   almost
last   next   sea   ✓let
school   hard   ✓began *begin*   above
father   ✓open   ✓grow   girl
✓keep   example   ✓took *take*   sometimes
tree   ✓begin   river   mountain
never   life   four   ✓cut
✓start   always   ✓carry   young
city   those   state   ✓talk
earth   both   once   soon
eye   paper   book   list
light   together   ✓hear   song
think ✓thought   ✓got *get*   stop   being *be*
head   group   without   ✓leave
under   often   second   family
story   ✓run   late   it's
See ✓saw   important   ✓miss   afternoon

Summary: Step 1

The Climate

Goal: To briefly explain to the student(s) *what* and *why*.

---

1. "I'm going to teach you to see letters in your imagination."

2. "It will help you read and spell words better."

3. "Here's how you can picture that."

4. Diagram a head with imagery for letters.

Summary:
Step 2
Imaging Letters

> **Goal:** Develop the ability to image, say, and write single letters by name and sound.

1. Imaging with a Letter Card
- Teacher shows a card with a single letter, for approximately two seconds.
- Student(s) says and writes the letter in the air, after the card is taken away.

2. Imaging without a Letter Card
- Teacher says a sound.
- Student(s) says and writes the letter in the air.

3. Keep in Mind
- Saying and air-writing should be simultaneous.
- Air-writing should be lower case.
- Air-writing should be large enough to see a *shadow effect*.
- If using the ADD Program, include the *labels* at any time.
- Include with any phonics program.
- Do some letter imagery in color.
- Overlap to other *Seeing Stars* steps by continuing this step and starting the simple level of another.

Group Stimulation

Stimulating symbol imagery for a small group or whole classroom requires no modification of the steps; rather, it requires group management. Have the group or class respond as a whole, and then check various students to make sure they are processing. Call on specific individuals and have the other students give thumbs up or thumbs down for agreement or not, producing more attentive, active participants.

Summary:
Step 3
Imaging Syllable Cards

> **Goal:** Develop the ability to image, write, and decode simple and complex nonsense words, including irregular spelling patterns.

1. Syllable Words are nonword single syllable words ranging from CV to CCVCC syllables, including irregularities such as ai, ea, oa, tch, ck, etc.

2. The structure of an English single syllable can be simple or complex:

Simple Syllables	*Complex Syllables*
CV	CCV
VC	VCC
CVC	CVCC
	CCVC
	CCVCC

3. Begin with simple syllable cards.

4. Lesson Summary:
   - Teacher shows syllable card , one second for each letter.
   - Student(s) sees, says letter names, and writes in the air.
   - Student(s) reads the nonword syllable from memory.
   - Saying letter names and writing should be done simultaneously.
   - Student(s) air-writes in lower case letters.
   - Student(s) air-writes *large enough* to see a "shadow" effect.

5. Error handle by responding to the response to give more opportunity to develop independent and rapid sensory-cognitive processing.

6. Pace by overlapping to the next Seeing Stars step, <u>Imaging and Sequencing Syllables</u> at a slightly lower level.

Group Stimulation

The <u>Imaging Syllable Cards</u> step can easily be used with a small group or whole classroom and *requires no modification of the process,* only group management techniques. Have the group or class respond as a whole, and then check various students to be sure they are imaging and air-writing appropriately. Call on specific individuals and have the other students give thumbs up or thumbs down to ensure active attention.

Summary:
Step 4

Imaging & Sequencing Syllables:
Syllable Board

> **Goal:** To develop symbol imagery for sequencing sounds in words, and beginning exposure to irregularities.

1. Student writes imaginary letters on the syllable board, starting from left to right.

2. The syllable board has designated units, place holders, for imaged letters.

3. Each letter has a separate space on the board, including digraphs, diphthongs, etc.

4. The stimulation moves from simple to complex syllables.

5. A chain of syllables is presented (one sound changing at time) to develop the hold and compare process.

6. Writing imaginary letters is less threatening than writing on paper!

7. Use common irregularities, such as the "final e" and "two vowels go walking" rule.

8. Pace by overlapping to the next step of Image and Air-Write at the same syllable level.

Lesson Summary:
Syllable Board

- Teacher says a syllable.

- Student(s) repeats the nonword syllable.

- Student(s) says and writes imaginary letters on the syllable board.

- Student(s) reads the nonword from memory.

- Teacher asks student(s) to recall a specific letter by its number in the syllable.

- Use "final e" and "two vowels go walking" rule.

- Remember:

    Saying letter names and writing should be done simultaneously.

    Student(s) writes in lower case letters.

    Student(s) writes large enough to see a "shadow" effect.

Group Instruction

Small or large group instruction does not require changing the steps for the syllable board stimulation. Each student has a board to use, whether in small groups or the entire class. Students choose the Syllable Board at the beginning of the lesson, or may have their own in their desk. As the teacher says the syllables, students are called on randomly for answers and other students give thumbs up or down to demonstrate their feedback to the response. Small groups of students often verbalize in unison, a small choir—fun if classroom teacher has previously established good control and rapport.

Summary:
Step 5

Imaging & Sequencing Syllables: Air-Writing *with* a Chain

> **Goal:** To develop symbol imagery for sounds within words from the simple through complex level, and teach visual memory for regularly irregular spelling patterns.

1. Student writes imaginary letters in the air.

2. A chain of syllables is presented to develop the hold and compare process.

3. The stimulation moves from simple to complex syllables.

4. Use common irregularities, such as "final e" and "two vowels go walking" rule, tch, dge, etc.

5. Stimulation starts with whole to parts, with teacher saying word and student imaging letters.

6. Stimulation moves to parts to whole, with teacher saying letters and student imaging word.

7. Use the phrase "see it and say it" when having students decode from imagery.

8. Do symbol imagery exercises:

• DECODE:	Student reads the syllable from the imaged pattern (memory).
• IDENTIFY:	Student identifies a specific letter from the imaged pattern.
• BACKWARDS:	Student says the letters backwards from the imaged pattern.
• MANIPULATE:	Student reads the syllable from imagery, after letters are manipulated.

Lesson Summary

- Teacher says syllables or letters in a chain, extending into CCVCC.
- Student(s) says and sometimes writes in the air, beginning to only imagine the letters, and thus hastening the lesson.
- Teacher randomly does the symbol imagery exercises:
    - Student(s) sees and says the word from memory.
    - Student(s) recalls a specific letter by its order in the syllable.
    - Student(s) says the letters backwards.
    - Student(s) sees and says the word after teacher manipulates the letters.
- Use English rules and expectancies to teach memory for how words are spelled.

Group Instruction

Small or large group instruction does not require changing the stimulation for the imaging and air-writing step. Each student does symbol imagery exercises or students are called on randomly for answers, using the thumbs up or down involvement. Small groups of students often verbalize the answer in unison. All in all, easy and fun.

Summary:
Step 6

Imaging & Sequencing Syllables:
Air-Writing *without* a Chain

> **Goal:** To develop symbol imagery for sounds/letters within words from the simple through complex level, and teach visual memory for regularly irregular spelling patterns.

1. Teacher says syllables or letters without a chain, a new word each time.

2. Student writes imaginary letters in the air.

3. The stimulation moves from simple to complex syllables.

4. From word to word all the sounds and letters change, no chaining.

5. Miscalling stimulates the hold and compare process.

6. Use common spelling irregularities.

7. Stimulation is mixed between whole to parts and parts to whole (word to letters or letters to word).

8. Do symbol imagery exercises:

   - DECODE: Student reads the syllable from the imaged pattern (memory).
   - IDENTIFY: Student identifies a specific letter from the imaged pattern.
   - BACKWARDS: Student says the letters backwards from the imaged pattern.
   - MANIPULATE: Student reads the syllable from imagery, after letters are manipulated.

Lesson Summary

- Teacher says syllables or letters without a chain, a new word each time, extending into complex syllables.
- Student(s) sees and says and sometimes writes in the air.
- Teacher miscalls the imaged word and student(s) judges and notes error.
- Symbol imagery exercises:
  - Student(s) sees and says the word from memory.
  - Student(s) recalls a specific letter by its order in the syllable.
  - Student(s) says the letters backwards.
  - Student(s) sees and says the word after teacher manipulates the letters.
- More focus on teaching spelling expectancies for memory of common spelling patterns.

Group Instruction

As with the previous step, small or large group instruction does not require change. Each student is given a word or letters to write in the air and/or does symbol imagery exercises. Continue thumbs up or down to demonstrate attention to the response. The miscalling activity is fun with students taking turns correcting the teacher's error. Perfect for working on vocabulary, sight words, spelling, terms, etc.

Summary: Step 7
Imaging Sight Words

> **Goal:** To build an extensive base of sight words, recognized instantly.

1. Capture and Categorize
   - Use a most commonly read list, such as the Fry list.
   - Capture the words not recognized immediately.
   - Put slow words on cards in lower case, bold letters.
   - Categorize the words into slow, medium, and fast piles.

2. Symbol image
   - Do symbol imagery exercises with sight words to place in visual memory.

3. Reinforce
   - Reinforce repetitively, moving words from slow to fast piles.
   - Use challenges to keep active attention and fun in reinforcement:
     — Wake Up and Put to Sleep
     — Read and Step
     — Tic Tac Toe and Read
     — Memory
     — Mine or Yours?
     — I'm a Card

Group Instruction

Establishing an extensive sight word base for each student is important, requiring capturing and categorizing his or her *own* sight words. Once this is completed, the same repetitive reinforcement applies. If there are five or six students such as Buzz in your class, this is an important area to give individualized attention. What else is going to make a significant difference in their lives? Not studying content, so replace a content activity with building the Visual Circle. If you can't, contact a local high school and bring in a work experience student to work daily with your students. Work experience students are free, must show up regularly, and this work may direct them toward a life of teaching.

When working with groups of students, capturing and categorizing may need to be with the collective group, with one box of sight words for the group. Repetitive reinforcement then requires you to be very observant regarding which words are difficult for which student, offering more stimulation to that student for given words. This is probably more difficult than setting up for individualized instruction!

Though specific words for specific students can't be reinforced, all the game-like challenges can be done with groups or classrooms of students. This is especially true for words in units, specific sight words you know need work, vocabulary words, terms from content, and spelling words. Words can be put on cards or on transparencies for the overhead projector—and become friends rather enemies.

Summary:
Step 8
Imaging, Reading & Spelling Two Syllables

> **Goal:** To develop symbol imagery for an instant base of spelling words, automatically extended during the act of reading.

1. Capture and Catalogue
  - Use most common spelling word list, such as Fry.
  - Capture the words not spelled instantly.
  - Put slow words on Visual Spelling Chart in lower case letters.
  - Catalogue the words on the chart to know which are able to be spelled instantly and which need more stimulation.

2. Analyze, Visualize, and Write on the Visual Spelling Chart
  - Student analyzes the word for phonetic irregularity.
  - Student marks the phonetic inconsistency, lightly so as not to disturb the visual pattern of the word.
  - Student visualizes the word, air-writing and saying letters.
  - Student writes the word on paper.
  - Student compares response to stimulus—uncovering stimulus and comparing with written response.

Group Instruction

Establishing an extensive spelling word base for each student is important, requiring capturing and cataloguing his or her spelling words on the Visual Spelling Chart (VSC). Once this is completed, the same repetitive reinforcement applies. Since this requires some individualized attention, this is another area requiring use of a class assistant such as a work experience student, parent volunteer, or even peer tutoring by a good speller in the class.

When working with groups of students, capturing and categorizing may need to be with the collective group, with one VSC for the group, though each student can keep a separate record of their difficult words. However, the technique of AVW is easily used with large or small groups, and is particularly fun with an overhead projector or chalkboard. The analysis part of the task can be done by specific students you have called on, thumbs up or down with others. Covering the analyzed word on the overhead or chalkboard, the visualizing and writing part of the activity can be with the whole group or class, each writing in the air at their desks and then writing on paper. Uncovering the word, each student can compare their writing to the stimulus word. My experience with classroom use of the AVW technique has been that words usually forgotten by the worst spellers, are magically and mysteriously remembered at the weekly spelling test.

Summary: Step 9

Imaging, Reading, & Spelling Two Syllables

> **Goal:** To develop symbol imagery for sequencing sounds/letters in two syllable words, and applying that processing to imaging, reading and spelling two syllable nonsense and real words.

1. Counting syllables:
   * Present concept that every syllable has a beat and a vowel letter.
   * Student(s) represents number of syllables by clapping or placing colored squares.

2. Teaching suffixes:
   * Present basic suffixes of le's, ly, tion, ture, ous, etc. to be stored and retrieved through imagery.
   * Suffixes are to be read and spelled instantly.
   * Add the remaining suffixes as appropriate, after beginning sequencing sounds/letters with the Multisyllable Board.
   * See the Appendix for a list of suffixes, or the *Seeing Stars* Kit for suffix cards.

3. Using the Multisyllable Board for sequencing sounds/letters:
   * Present the syllables in a chain, either changing a letter or a suffix.
   * Use chains that focus on changing the letter just prior to the suffix.
   * Student(s) says, images, and writes each chunk on the Multisyllable Board.
   * Do symbol imagery exercises for each chunk.
   * Do symbol imagery exercises for the whole word, chunk by chunk.
   * Be sure symbol imagery is consistent with English spelling rules.

4. Breaking suggestions:
- Present and practice three basic breaking rules:
  — Find and break in front of an ending.
  — Find and break between double letters.
  — Start a syllable with a consonant, if you can.
- Teach the open/closed syllable rule for reading and spelling.
- The vowel says its name if open next to the syllable line.
- The vowel says its sound if closed next to the syllable line.

5. Breaking, reading, and imaging two syllable words:
- Student(s) reads and images two syllable cards, changing one card at a time. Do this only for a short introductory time, or not at all.
- Be careful to create words consistent with English.
- Practice open/closed syllable decoding.
- Student(s) breaks, reads and images two syllable words from lists or cards.
- Marks the syllable with a light, diagonal line.
- Reads each chunk, may identify the suffix first, but puts word together front to back.
- Images chunks.
- Practice open/closed syllable decoding.
- Do symbol imagery exercises for chunks of the word, specific letters, or whole word (chunk by chunk).
- Use nonsense words to improve phonetic processing.
- Use real words to extend instant word recognition base.

6. Imaging, writing, and breaking for spelling two syllable words:
- Student(s) spells two syllable words from lists or cards.
- Counts syllables first.
- Says the chunks.
- Images the chunks.
- Writes the chunks.
- Marks the syllables with a light, diagonal line.
- Checks response by touching and saying each chunk.
- Practice open/closed syllable rule.
- Do symbol imagery exercises for chunks of the word, specific letters, or whole word (chunk by chunk).
- Use nonsense words to improve phonetic processing.
- Use real words to extend memorized spelling base.

7. Teacher miscalls and student(s) monitors and corrects.

Group Instruction

Small or large group instruction does not require changing the steps for two syllable stimulation. Each student has a Multisyllable Board to use, whether in small groups or the entire class. As the teacher says the syllables, students are called on randomly for answers and other students give thumbs up or down to demonstrate their feedback to the response.

Suffix cards can be kept on large cards for group or classroom use, or put on 3X5 cards for each student and kept in individualized plastic index card holders to be practiced for instant reading and spelling. Group lessons can be: 1) teacher says a suffix, students find it in suffix array and hold it up, 2) all students put the suffix card down with one student called on to image, say, and air-write the letters, 3) remaining students give thumbs up or down, 4) all students air-write the letters, 5) teacher holds up the suffix card and all students read it, 6) teacher holds up the card and a designated student reads it.

Reading two syllable words can be accomplished at the chalkboard or on the overhead projector. Break, read, and image as a group or with designated students. Students can hold enlarged core and suffix cards, come to the front of the room and create patterns to be read. Spelling two syllable words can first be done individually within the group, with students saying, air-writing, writing, and breaking at their desks; the writing and breaking can also be done at the chalkboard or on the overhead projector.

Summary:
Step 10

Imaging, Reading & Spelling Three Syllables

> **Goal:** To develop symbol imagery for sequencing sounds/letters in three syllable words, and applying that processing to imaging, reading and spelling three syllable nonsense and real words.

1. Teaching prefixes:
   - Present basic prefixes of pre, pro, con, dis, ex, trans, etc., to be stored and retrieved through imagery.
   - Prefixes are to be read and spelled instantly.
   - Add the remaining prefixes as appropriate, after beginning sequencing sounds/letters with the Multisyllable Board.
   - See the Appendix for a list of prefixes or the *Seeing Stars* Kit for prefix cards.

2. Using the Multisyllable Board for sequencing sounds/letters in three syllables:
   - Present the syllables in a chain, either changing a letter or an affix, but not both.
   - Use chains that focus on changing the letter just prior to the suffix.
   - Student(s) says, images, and writes each chunk on the Multisyllable Board.
   - Do symbol imagery exercises for each chunk.
   - Do symbol imagery exercises for the whole word, chunk by chunk.
   - Be sure symbol imagery is consistent with English spelling rules.

3. Breaking, reading, and imaging three syllable words:
- Student(s) reads and images three syllable cards, changing one card at a time. Do this only for a short introductory time, or not at all.
- Be careful to create words consistent with English.
- Practice open/closed syllable decoding.
- Student(s) breaks, reads and images three syllable words from lists or cards.
  — Find and mark the syllable with a light, diagonal line.
  — Image chunks.

4. Imaging, spelling, and breaking three syllable words:
- Student(s) says, images, spells three syllable words.
  — Student counts syllables first.
  — Student(s) may need to write each syllable on a designated line for extra support.
  — Student follows the pattern of: say, image, write, break, and check.
- Do symbol imagery exercises for chunks of the word, specific letters, or whole word (chunk by chunk).

Group Instruction

Small or large group instruction does not require changing the steps for three syllable stimulation. Each student may have a Multisyllable Board, whether in small groups or in the classroom. When the teacher says the syllables, students are called on randomly for answers and other students give thumbs up or down to demonstrate their feedback to the response.

As with the suffix cards, prefix cards can be kept for the group, on large cards for classroom use, or also put on 3X5 cards for each student and placed in individualized plastic index card holders to be practiced for instant reading and spelling. As with suffix stimulation, small and large group practice for instant recognition for prefixes requires group management, keeping the lesson interesting and focused on the task of imagery and reinforcement. Flash the prefixes for group reading since prefixes are easier and shorter than suffixes; but, it is important to call on a "Buzz" to image the letters, ensuring his participation and development.

As with two syllables, reading three syllable words can be fun at the chalkboard or on the overhead projector. Break, read, and image as a group or with designated students. Students can hold enlarged core and affix cards, come to the front of the room and create patterns to be read. Spelling three syllable words can first be done individually within the group, with students saying, air-writing, writing, and breaking at their desks. The writing and breaking can also be done at the chalkboard or on the overhead projector.

Bibliography

References

Adams, M.J. (1990). *Beginning to read: Thinking and learning about print.* Cambridge, MA: Press.

Aristotle. (1972). *Aristotle on memory.* Providence, Rhode Island: Brown University Press.

Arnheim, R. (1966). Image and thought. In G. Kepes (Ed.). *Sign, image, symbol.* New York: George Braziller, Inc.

Ball, E.W., & Blachman, B.A. (1991). Does phoneme awareness training in kindergarten make a difference in early word recognition and developmental spelling? *Reading Research Quarterly, 26,* 49-66.

Barker, T.A., Torgesen, J.K., & Wagner, R.K.. (1992). The role of orthographic processing skills on five different reading tasks. *Reading Research Quarterly.*

Barron, R. (1986). Word recognition in early reading: A review of the direct and indirect access hypothesis. Cognition, 24, 93-119.

Barron, R. (1981a). Reading skill and reading strategies. In A. Lesgold & C. Perfetti (Eds.), Interactive processes in reading. Hillsdale, NJ: Earlbaum.

Bell, N. (1991). Gestalt imagery: a critical factor in language comprehension. *Annals of Dyslexia,* 41, 246-260.

Bell, N. (1991). *Visualizing and verbalizing for language comprehension and thinking.* Paso Robles: Academy of Reading Publications.

Berninger, V. (1986). Normal variation in reading acquisition. Perceptual and Motor Skills, 62, 691-716.

Bleasdale, F. (1983). Paivio's dual-coding model of meaning revisited. In J.C. Yuille (Ed.), *Imagery, memory and cognition: Essays in honor of Allan Paivio.* New Jersey: Lawrence Erlbaum Associates.

Calfee, R., Lindamood, C. & Lindamood, P. (1973). Acoustic-phonetic skills and reading-kindergarten through twelfth grade. *Journal of Educational Psychology.* 64, 293-298.

Farah, M. J. (1984). The neurological basis of mental imagery: A componential analysis. *Cognition*.

Fry, E. (1994). 1000 Instant Words: The Most Common Words for Teaching Reading, Writing and Spelling. Laguna Beach, CA: Laguna Beach Educational Books.

Foss, D.J. (1988). Experimental psycholinguistics. In M.R. Rosenzweig & L.W. Porter (Eds.), *Annual Review of Psychology*, Vol. 39. Palo Alto, CA: Annual Reviews Inc.

Frith, U. (1985). Beneath the surface of developmental dyslexia. In K. Patterson, J. Marshall, & M. Coltheart (Eds.), *Surface dyslexia* . London: Erlbaum.

Haines, L. P., & Leong, C.K. (1983). Coding processes in skilled and less skilled readers. *Annals of Dyslexia,* Vol. 33. Baltimore, MD: Orton Dyslexia Society.

Hammill, D. D. *Detroit Tests of Learning Aptitude*. Austin Texas: PRO-ED.

Harris, A. J. & Sipay, E.R. (1990). *How to Increase Reading Ability.* New York: Longman.

Healy, Jane M. (1990). *Endangered minds: Why our children don't think.* Simon & Schuster.

Kaluger G., & Kolson, C.J. (1969). *Reading and Learning Disabilities.* Columbus, Ohio: Charles E. Merrill Publishing Company.

Katz, L., & Feldmean, L. (1981). Linguistic coding in word recognition: Comparisons between a deep and a shallow orthography. In A. Lesgold & C. Perfetti (Eds.), Interactive processes in reading (pp. 85-106). Hillsdale, NJ: Laurence Erlbaum.

Kippling, R. (1959). If. *The Golden Treasury of Poetry.* New York: Western Publishing Co.

Kleiman, G.M., & Humphrey, M. M. (1982). *Phonological representations in visual word recognition: The adjunct access model.* Technical Report No. 247. Champaign, IL: Center for the Study of Reading, University of Illinois.

Kosslyn, S.M. & Koenig, O. (1992). *Wet Mind, The New Cognitive Neuroscience.* New York: The Free Press: A division of Macmillan, Inc.

Kosslyn, S.M. (1976). Using imagery to retrieve semantic information: A developmental study. *Child Development* 47:434-444.

Lee, Harper. (1960). *To Kill a Mockingbird.*

Liberman, I. & Shankweiler, D. (1985). Phonology and the problems of learning to read and write. *Remedial and Special Education, 6,* 8-17.

Lindamood, P. (1985). *Cognitively developed phonemic awareness as a base for literacy.* Paper presented at the National Reading Conference, San Diego, CA., December.

Lindamood, C.H., & Lindamood, P.C. (1979). *Lindamood® Auditory Conceptualization (LAC)Test.* Austin: PRO-ED.

Lindamood, C.H., & Lindamood, P.C. (1975). *Auditory discrimination in depth.* Austin: PRO-ED.

Linden, M.A. and Witrock, M.C. (1981). The teaching of reading comprehension according to the model of generative learning. *Reading Research Quarterly* 17,:44-57.

Long, S.A., and Winograd, P.N., and Bridge, C.A. (1989). The effects of reader and text characteristics on reports of imagery during and after reading. *Reading Research Quarterly* 19(3):353-372.

Lundberg. I. (1988). Preschool prevention of reading failure: Does training in phonological awareness work: In R.L. Masland and M.W. Masland (Eds.). *Prevention of reading failure.* (pp. 163-176) Parkton, MD: York Press.

Lundberg, I., Frost, J., & Peterson, O. (1988). Effects of an extensive program for stimulating phonological awareness in pre-school children. *Reading Research Quarterly, 23,* 263-284.

Oliver, M.E. (1967). Initial Perception of Word Forms. *Elementary English*

Oliver, M.E. (1982). Improving comprehension with mental imagery. Paper read at the annual Meeting of the Washington Organization for Reading Development of the International Reading Association, Seattle, Washington , March 1982.

Olsen, R., Forsberg, H., Wise, B., & Rack, J. (1994) Measurement of word recognition, orthographic, and phonological skills. In G.R. Lyon (Ed.). *Frames of reference for the assessment of learning disabilities* (pp. 243- 277). Baltimore, MD: Brookes Publishing.

Paivio, A. (1969). Mental imagery in associative learning and memory. *Psychological Review* 76:241-263.

Paivio, A. (1971). *Imagery and verbal processes.* New York: Holt, Rinehart, and Winston. Reprinted 1979. Hillsdale NJ: Lawrence Erlbaum Associates.

Paivio, A. (1986). *Mental representations: A dual coding approach.* New York: Oxford University Press.

Paivio, A. (1996). Presentation at the National Lindamood-Bell Research and Training Conference, San Francisco, California.

Pribram, K. (1971). *Languages of the brain: Experimental paradoxes and principles in neuropsychology.* New York: Brandon House, Inc.

Sadoski, M. (1983). An exploratory study of the relationship between reported imagery and the comprehension and recall of a story. *Reading Research Quarterly* 19(1):110-123.

Shankweiler, D., & Liberman, I.Y. (1989). *Phonology and reading disability.* Ann Arbor: University of Michigan Press.

Simons, H.D., & Leu, Jr., D.J. (1987). The Use of Contextual and graphic information in word recognition by second-, fourth-, and sixth-grade readers. *Journal of Reading Behavior.*

Smith, F. (1928). *Understanding Reading: A Psycholinguistic Analysis of Reading and Learning to Read.* New York: Holt, Rinehart and Winston.

Stanovich, K.E. (1991). Changing models of reading and reading acquisition. In Rieben, L. & Perfetti, C.A. (Eds.), *Learning to read: Basic research and its implications* (pp. 19-32). Hillsdale, NJ: Lawrence Erlbaum Associates.

Stanovich, K.E. (1980). Toward an interactive-compensatory model of individual differences in the development of reading fluency. *Reading Research Quarterly,* 16, 32-71.

Torgesen, J., Morgan, S. & Davis, C. (1992). The effects of two types of phonological awareness training on word learning in kindergarten children. *Journal of Educational Psychology, 84,* 364-370.

Torgesen, J., Wagner, B. & Rashotte, C. (1996). Approaches to the prevention and remediation of phonologically based reading disabilities. In B. Blachman (Ed.) *Cognitive and Linguistic Foundations of Reading Acquisition: Implications for Intervention Research.* Hillsdale, NJ: Erlbaum.

Wagner, R.K., Torgesen, J.K., & Rashotte, C.A. (1994). The development of reading-related phonological processing abilities: New evidence of bi-directional causality from a latent variable longitudinal study. *Developmental Psychology, 30:* 73-87.